m

gift

DATE DUE

APR 2 9 2003

THE MARRANO LEGACY

THE

MARRANO LEGACY

A Contemporary Crypto-Jewish Priest

Reveals Secrets of His Double Life

TRUDI ALEXY

UNIVERSITY OF NEW MEXICO PRESS

ALBUQUERQUE

In ever cherished memory of George,

who taught me so much

about life, love, and faith

LIBRARY OF CONGRESS CATALOGING-IN-PUBLICATION DATA

Alexy, Trudi.
The Marrano legacy : a contemporary crypto-Jewish priest reveals
secrets of his double life / Trudi Alexy.
p. cm.
ISBN 0-8263-3055-X (cloth : alk. paper)
1. Simon—Religion. 2. Simon—Correspondence. 3. Marranos—Latin
America—Religious life. 4. Marranos—Latin America—Social life and
customs. 5. Priests—Latin America. 6. Alexy, Trudi—Correspondence.
7. Alexy, Trudi—Religion. 8. Jews—Identity. 9. Jews—Cultural
assimilation. 10. Latin America—Ethnic relations. I. Title.

F1419.J4 A39 2003
296.8'3—dc21

2002151376

Design: Mina Yamashita

Contents

Acknowledgments

My deepest appreciation to my agent, Julie Popkin, for her sensitivity and encouragement, and to Dr. Stanley Hordes, for his steadfast support and generous efforts on my behalf.

My sincere thanks to other historians and experts whose knowledge and scholarship contributed so much to my research: Dr. Janet Liebman Jacobs, Professor Eduardo Días, Dr. David Gitlitz, Benjamin Nachman, and Arthur Benveniste.

Enormous gratitude to Luther Wilson, director of University of New Mexico Press, and David Holtby, editor in chief and associate director at the press, who had the courage to champion such a controversial book. A most special thanks to editor Evelyn Schlatter at UNM Press, who brought my book to their attention and without whose enthusiastic endorsement, persistence, and humor I might have given up trying to get this book published. She made me laugh while hanging tough.

But my most heartfelt thanks go to all who trusted me with their stories, particularly to Simon, who risked so much to help his people. I will forever treasure his friendship.

FOREWORD

STANLEY HORDES, PH.D.
—Cofounder of the Society of Crypto-Judaic Studies and Former
President of the New Mexico Jewish Historical Society

I first met Trudi Alexy in January of 1991. We both were attending a conference in Tucson, Arizona, on the history of Crypto-Judaism in the U.S. Southwest. I was beginning to conduct research into the history of a group of people within the Hispanic community in New Mexico who claimed to have descended from the original conversos, those Jews who, in the 1490s, were forced to convert from Judaism to Catholicism.

During the course of my archival research, I had examined hundreds of Inquisition trial records from Mexico and Spain and was able to discern from them the emotional torment experienced by the children, grandchildren, and great-grandchildren of those fifteenth-century conversos.

Conversations with the twentieth-century descendants of these individuals revealed a wide range of consciousness about their past, from vague notions of a Jewish ancestor, to practices suggestive of a Jewish origin, to outright acknowledgment by a grandparent. But after five centuries of living in secret, whatever had been handed down from generation to generation had often undergone significant transformation, borrowing much from the dominant Christian culture in which these descendants of the Crypto-Jews had lived.

As Ms. Alexy began relating her personal story to me during this initial meeting in 1991, chills ran down my spine. Here was a twentieth-century conversa relating the story of the denial by her assimilated family of her Jewish heritage during her childhood, her hasty conversion to Catholicism as an adolescent to escape Hitler's persecution on the eve of World War II, and her coming to terms with the conflicts in her life as an adult. This was, I believed, as close as I was ever going to come to visiting with one of my

FOREWORD

"subjects" from fifteenth-century Spain.

A decade later, I experienced the same chills as I read the draft of the first chapter of this book, as Ms. Alexy described the initial conflict of accepting baptism at the age of eleven, knowing it was wrong to deny her Judaism while, at the same time, understanding the necessity to save her life and that of her family.

I read of the guilt, the repression, the shame, and the anxieties she experienced, the feelings of marginality in both the Jewish and Catholic worlds, and I compared these emotions with those articulated by the defendants in the centuries-old Inquisition trials, as well as by their twentieth-century descendants.

This book relates the story of Ms. Alexy's relationships with two Crypto-Jewish priests, "Matthew" and "Simon," one in the United States, the other in Latin America. During the course of her discussions with these individuals, she elicits from them a spectrum of conflicting emotions that often results from leading such a dual life: fear of recognition, anger at being constantly and unfairly judged, ambivalence about revealing one's true identity, and the desire to someday live openly as a Jew.

Trudi Alexy is neither a professional historian nor is she trained as an anthropologist; thus the reader of her book should not judge her work according to the academic standards of these disciplines. But as a psycho-therapist, Ms. Alexy offers far more than the sterile analysis of cause-and-effect relationships, and she elicits from "Matthew" and "Simon" more profound insights than could any social scientist. It is precisely because she emerged from a similar background as her subjects that she is able to gain their trust and, with their permission, share their moving stories with us in this volume.

I

Prologue

This is the story of an intensely personal relationship between two strangers who established a deep spiritual bond because they share a unique experience: both did not discover they were Jews until they were in their teens. Both hid their Jewishness and lived as Catholics to escape persecution in opposite ends of the world.

She was going to be a nun. He became a priest. She now lives openly as a Jew. He has lived the hazardous life of a Crypto (hidden)-Jewish Catholic priest, providing protection to a large community of secret Jews living as Catholics south of the U.S. border.

Those who know nothing about their history might well wonder why thousands of Jews, whose ancestors left Spain centuries ago, still hide their true identities under a Christian cover, here, on the American continent, five hundred years after the start of the Inquisition, fifty years after the Holocaust.

During the past decade much has been written about Crypto-Jews, descendants of Spain's medieval Marranos, Jews who converted under duress but lived as secret Jews, passing on their ancient laws and traditions from one generation to the next.

I am using the word Marranos here only because it remains the most familiar one by which those Jewish converts-in-name-only are still known today, although it is a derisive, insulting name meaning "swine."

Medieval Christians who never accepted the newly baptized Jews as true Catholics first called them Marranos, but so did nonbaptized Jews, who reviled them as apostates and accused them of betraying their own people by becoming Christians.

I should stress here that even highly regarded historians often disagree not only over the interpretation and veracity of the information that has been reported about contemporary Crypto-Jews, whose very existence is sometimes called into question, but about the secret practices and observances of the Marranos. Because secrecy has been so central to their survival, most of their history continues to be transmitted orally. Thus it is sometimes impossible to provide conventional proof documenting and authenticating their stories.

Because statistics vary greatly, as do accounts of their persecution, some historians find it easy to dismiss them as exaggerated and even as myths.

Some of those skeptics have become increasingly vocal, publishing numerous articles attacking the credibility of the researchers whose findings they dispute.

This has deterred neither the researchers nor a great many ordinary Christians who have found sufficient reasons to suspect from various familial clues that their ancestors might have been secret Jews and are doing genealogical studies on their own to unravel the mysteries of their past.

What has resulted from all this exploration is a clearer, much more detailed picture explaining the causes, reasons, and motives behind the pervasive, even obsessive secrecy among present-day descendants of those earlier Crypto-Jews.

Since I am not a historian, the sources I have most relied on for information were researchers who have spent years investigating Inquisition records and other archival documents, as well as diaries, letters, and oral histories collected by them and by myself. Personal interviews with those who claimed to be descendants of the Marranos were particularly revealing. They related stories about everyday life as well as accounts of traumatic events in the lives of their ancestors passed on to them by parents, grandparents, and great-grandparents, sometimes supported by legal documents and photographs, shedding light on odd heretofore hidden familial customs and practices. Most importantly, they also disclosed how they coped with the difficulties of living dual lives, their own near paranoid fear of exposure and continued commitment to hiding their true identities.

I anticipate that this nontraditional approach to history is bound to arouse some controversy, because, despite my efforts to remain objective, I have been influenced by my personal connection to the two Crypto-Jewish priests whose experiences, shared here with my readers, often mirrored my own. But as a psychotherapist, I have been equally affected by my focus on the emotional and spiritual influences that have so dramatically distorted the lives of these extraordinary people.

For those researchers who have recently begun to investigate the Crypto-Jews' lifestyles, traditions, and belief systems, eliciting disclosures from them has not been an easy task.

When confronted with questions from anyone who suspects or has discovered some clues to the Crypto-Jews' true identities, they deny everything. Even most former members who have come out openly as Jews shun publicity and evade any inquiry about their people.

In 1991, soon after I had accidentally stumbled on the existence of Crypto-Jews during my research for my first book, The Mezuzah in the Madonna's Foot, I was invited to attend the International Conference on the Inquisition and the Hidden Jews of the Southwest, in Tucson, Arizona.

To my surprise it was attended by many U.S. researchers, historians, and professors and their colleagues from foreign universities. Their scholarly presentations showed how widespread the curiosity and fascination with the heretofore almost unknown Crypto-Jews had become.

I joined the newly established Society for Crypto-Judaic Studies, whose cofounder is Professor Stanley Hordes, Ph.D., author of the forthcoming *To the End of the World: The History of the Crypto-Jews of New Mexico.* He and David Gitlitz, Ph.D., author of Secrecy and Deceit: The Religion of the Crypto-Jews, are by many considered to be among the foremost authorities on the subject. It is also true that they disagree about many of their respective findings and conclusions.

In addition to the many articles that have appeared for the past twenty years in a variety of mainstream publications as well as in academic journals, the society produces its own quarterly magazine, Halapid (The Torch), and holds yearly conferences where new information is shared.

The Public Broadcast System and National Public Radio have produced and sponsored several audio and video documentaries on the Crypto-Jews, which, due to repeated airings, managed to reach a wide and varied audience and quickly created a veritable groundswell of interest.

Shortly after my first book was published, PBS taped an interview with me. Due to a lucky oversight, a New York Radio station ran that dialogue three times in one day.

Because these broadcasts were unscheduled and thus unlisted, many viewers came upon them by accident. This resulted in an unusually large number of callers to the station, asking for information because they had missed the beginning, which identified me as the author, and the name of my book. Despite the fact that only the last forty pages of The Mezuah in the Madonna's Foot deal with secret Jews, most asked where they could get the book "about the Crypto-Jews"!

It was this and other evidence of growing interest that prompted Harper/San Francisco, who published the paperback edition of my book in 1994, to add Marranos and Other Secret Jews to its subtitle.

Most Jews who refused to convert and were forced by the Expulsion Decree of 1492 to leave Spain fled to France, Italy, Portugal, and the Ottoman Empire, among other countries.

However, it is a well-documented historical fact that those who remained in Spain, expecting to be left in peace once they submitted to the Church's demands, found out that baptism proved to be an insufficient and unreliable protection against zealous Inquisitors who refused to trust the new converts and continued to harass and threaten them.

Thus thousands of "converted" Jews soon fled to foreign lands, hoping to live openly as Jews wherever they felt safe enough to risk it. But memories of past persecutions and fear of their recurrence convinced many of these people to continue hiding their true identities.

This is particularly true of those who followed Christopher Columbus west across the Atlantic to the New World as newly baptized Catholics. Hoping to leave their tormented lives behind, they were determined to

Prologue

conceal their ancestral Jewish practices and thus became Crypto-Jews.

Today their descendants live in various-sized clusters throughout Mexico and Central and South America, as well as all over the North American Southwest: Colorado, Texas, New Mexico, Arizona, and California.

Until now, most of what we know about present-day Crypto-Jews—their beliefs, their practices and justification for their continued secrecy—has come from formerly hidden members. They have risked everything: banishment from their communities and rejection by their families, including threats to their very lives, to leave their secret lives behind and openly "come out" as Jews.

This book provides an unprecedented insight into the reasons that would compel "Simon," a deeply religious contemporary Jew, to carry on his people's ancient tradition of secrecy while living his outer life as a Catholic priest.

Although I have Simon's full name and permission to use his letters in this book, I must honor his request that he remain anonymous here for reasons that became clear at the start of our lengthy and candid correspondence. Reading his letters offers an eerie glimpse into a present-day anachronism. This anachronism has its roots in the Spanish Inquisition, which began at the end of the fifteenth century.

At that time the victorious armies of Spain's Catholic monarchs, Queen Isabella and King Ferdinand, had finally recaptured all of the lands conquered by the Moors (Muslims, Islamic followers of the prophet Mohammed) during the preceding eight centuries.

The history of the Jews in Spain is full of controversy and contradictions. It also sounds strangely familiar, like an echo from the past recurring again and again. . . .

Despite the fact that Jews lived in Spain before either the Christians or the Moors, it is not surprising that they were easy scapegoats and always vulnerable to the political and economic whims of the ruling majority, because Jews never governed any of the land nor commanded armies of their own.

The Moorish conquest of Spain, launched from North Africa in a.d. 711, ushered in a tug-of-war between the separate Christian and Moorish kingdoms that did not end until 1492, when the Moslems abandoned all hope of holding on to their last stronghold at the great fortress of the Alhambra in Granada and surrendered to the Catholic monarchs' armies. That date also spelled the end of the Jews' visible presence in Spain.

But until then, during the eight-hundred-year-long on-again, off-again struggle for control over the Iberian Peninsula, interspersed by years of peaceful and productive coexistence, Jews managed to maintain a working relationship with both warring factions.

Although the majority of Jews earned a meager living as laborers and tradesmen, many of the more educated Jews prospered in professions and in business, owned land, and often attained positions of great power and influence in the courts of their Christian and Moorish rulers.

During those many centuries, this cooperation between members of the three major monotheistic religions blossomed into the Golden Age of Spain, often referred to as the "Era of Conviviencia" (coexistence), and is acknowledged as the precursor of the great European Renaissance.

Jews collaborated with Christians and Moors to create literature, philosophy, and science unequaled in volume and quality anywhere else in the world during that era. They excelled in translating the great works of Greek, Roman, Arabic, and Hebrew scholars. Together they helped bring Spain to the world's cultural pinnacle.

Major cities like Cordoba, Granada, Sevilla, Toledo, Barcelona, and Gerona had renowned centers of learning supported by flourishing Jewish communities. The names of Yehuda Halevy, Moses Maimonedes, Abraham Zacuto, Moses Nahmanides, Abraham ibn Ezra, and Shlomo ibn Gabirol will, in the words of Spain's King Juan Carlos I, "be inscribed in golden letters in the books of literature, philosophy, and science" (in his letter to the author, dated August 23, 1991).

But as the Christians slowly reconquered the lands occupied by the Moors, the fate of the Jews changed dramatically.

Persecution in the form of psychological pressure as well as forced baptisms under threat of torture and death, although officially discouraged by the Church, increased in intensity.

Mobs, whipped into murderous frenzy by fanatical preachers, slaughtered, plundered, and destroyed entire Jewish communities long before 1478, when Queen Isabella and King Ferdinand finally persuaded Pope Innocent VIII to set up the Church's watchdog tribunal, the Inquisition, to ensure and protect Spain's Catholic "purity."

For Spanish Jews, 1492 proved to be the most momentous year. Tomas de Torquemada, the Catholic Church's Grand Inquisitor, though widely assumed to have been born a Jew, became convinced that Judaism was "an incurable disease" and feared that unbaptized Jews were contaminating the new converts.

He persuaded the queen that the best way to secure the Catholic integrity of her realm was to commit herself to the ideal of "one people, one kingdom, one faith."

The only way to achieve this sacred goal was to rid Spain of all unrepentant infidels: force every non-Catholic to convert.

The Expulsion Decree of 1492 gave those Jews refusing baptism three months to settle their affairs and, abandoning everything of value, to leave Spain forever. The alternative was death by fire.

On February 12, 1502, Queen Isabella issued a Royal Order giving thousands of Moors the same choice as the earlier Expulsion Decree gave the Jews: convert or leave Spain.

After being an integral part of Spanish life for so many centuries, approximately half of Spain's 200,000 to 300,000 Jews chose to flee rather than submit to religious blackmail.

Many left behind prosperous commercial holdings, vast estates with orchards and vineyards that were immediately appropriated and divided between the Crown and the Church.

They fled west to neighboring Portugal, south to North Africa, east to Italy, Turkey, Greece, and the Balkans, as well as the New World.

The poor Jews who had chosen to emigrate, with little to lose, left mostly for economic reasons, hoping to find not only safety but better opportunities elsewhere. Once settled, a good percentage of them soon became assimilated into the Catholic mainstream.

By the seventeenth century, many of those who had remained in Spain, believing they would be safe if they professed to be Catholic, found their hopes dashed and decided to leave. In addition to following the emigration paths chosen by those who had fled earlier, a large number of the new emigrants now moved north to the Netherlands.

They were allowed to take with them only what they could carry, with the exception of gold coins, jewelry, and other such portable treasures, which were so valuable that the Church leaders were unwilling to let them slip through their fingers. They confiscated the loot and added it to their own coffers.

Despite the hardship they would have to face, those Jews who left primarily for religious reasons stubbornly refused to abjure their faith or allow anyone to deprive them of their culture, their professional and business know-how, or their language (a mixture of ancient Spanish, Portuguese, Arabic, and Hebrew), integrating indigenous words and idioms as they moved from country to country. This language evolved over time survives to this day among Sephardic Jews as Ladino just as Yiddish evolved for Ashkenazic Jews.

With all the infidels banished, it appeared that all the separate Spanish kingdoms on the Iberian Peninsula would at long last be united under one faith and one flag. The Church was determined to keep it that way.

The Inquisition soon moved to neighboring Portugal after Spain refused to allow a member of the impoverished Portuguese royal family to marry into their own unless they got rid of their native Jews as well as those who had only recently fled there to escape the Spanish Church's persecution.

But by then Portugal had learned a painful lesson from their neighbor's experience: the Expulsion Decree had robbed Spain of thousands of talented, productive citizens. The Portuguese were determined not to repeat that mistake.

Instead of expelling the recalcitrant Jews, they gathered them all together, forced them to convert, and passed a law allowing them to marry only into "old Catholic" families.

Many Jews refused to obey this draconian law. Several families left their homes and settled in small hamlets high in the Portuguese mountains, where they remained hidden for centuries, far from the Inquisition's scrutiny.

They pretended to be Christians while holding on to their ancient Jewish traditions in secret. While other villagers sometimes suspected something was odd about them, no one was able to prove anything.

Only recently, in one such village, Belmonte, over one hundred secret Jews decided to shed their Catholic cover after many generations had lived hiding their true identities. Together they emerged from the shadow of fear: the men were circumcised, the women submitted to purification in the mikvah, and a rabbi from Israel responded to their call for help and came to minister to this small flock.

As news of their emergence into the open reached beyond Belmonte, the world was amazed to find that major elements of the Crypto-Jews' ancient beliefs, traditions, and rituals had been preserved by them for nearly five centuries.

▼

Despite the risks involved, an estimated 100,000 to 150,000 Jews defied the Expulsion Decree and refused to leave Spain. After all, Spain had been their home for many generations.

Although the majority of Jews struggled to support their families like any ordinary Spaniard, eking out a spare living as farmers, laborers, and tradesmen, most were relatively content with their lot. However, many of the more educated Jews had achieved substantial financial success and were respected in the medical, financial, and academic professions. With so much to lose, although persecution remained a threat for all Jews who chose to stay in Spain, living with it was a risk most were willing to accept.

Jews knew even before 1492 that many Spanish laws discriminated against them, but they learned to live with them by devising shrewd ways to circumvent them.

Despite the existence of laws that were supposed to protect Jewish rights to own land, unscrupulous officials who coveted a Jew's property often ignored those laws. If one of them came to a Jew whose family owned vineyards and convinced him that he would not be allowed to keep his property unless he became a Catholic, one member of the family agreed to get baptized. Sole ownership of the vineyard was transferred to him, but at least it was still in the family. The "convert" made certain no one knew that he and his family continued to maintain their religious practices in secret.

When the Expulsion Decree was passed, Jews were certain that this latest outburst of anti-Judaism, like so many previous ones, would eventually simmer down, only to flare up again, here and there, temporarily fanned to combustion by another fanatical, Jew-hating cleric. Had this not always been the pattern of their lives, and had not enough of them survived these life-threatening firestorms to make remaining in Spain worth the gamble?

So, when the Church offered them an alternative, "convert or leave," many Jews chose baptism, took their Jewish beliefs, practices, and traditions underground, and remained in Spain.

After all, they did not take seriously the ritual or the vow they were forced to make. Jews knew that the Kol Nidre, an ancient Aramaic prayer traditionally part of services on Yom Kippur, the Day of Atonement, allowed them to ask G-d to forgive them for any false religious vows made during the year if they felt their lives were in jeopardy. Judging from their history, when was a Jew's life not in danger? And besides, what did a little holy water mean to a Jew? So, the "converts" simply chose to do whatever Spanish law required of them in order to survive in their homeland.

But it was easy to see why newly baptized Jews never felt safe, no matter how hard they tried to escape harassment and persecution by blending into Spanish society.

Suspicious "Old Catholics" never trusted or accepted the new "Conversos." They also never tired of spying on them and needed little reason to accuse them of "judaizing": continuing to practice their customs and rituals in secret and trying to convert Christians with whom they came into contact.

Prologue

Except for some efforts to bring those who had been forced to convert back into the fold, Jews have traditionally avoided proselytizing. After choosing baptism as the only way to evade expulsion and survive in Spain, they kept their forbidden religious practices well hidden. They were not about to call any undue attention to themselves by trying to convince Old Christians to join their ranks.

Like the Jews who had chosen to remain in Spain after submitting to baptism-in-name-only, many of the Marranos who had fled to the New World also felt it was too dangerous to abandon their Christian mask. They learned to cleverly disguise their traditions and customs, to celebrate their holidays in ways that would make detection unlikely, and passed on their secret ways from one generation to the next.

Dr. Janet Liebman Jacobs, writing about contemporary Crypto-Jewish observances in the Journal for the Scientific Study of Religion, cites research findings of several experts in this field (Santos, Fernandez, Nidel). She quotes an anonymous person who described the way some secret Jews practiced the ritual of lighting Sabbath candles without calling attention to themselves: each Friday his mother paid the local church keeper to light two candles high up on the altar and keep the oil well filled. Since it was done in a church, no one accused her of being a "Sabadista," one who celebrates the Sabbath.

Purim, the Fast of Queen Esther, is the most popular holiday for Crypto-Jews. It celebrates the heroism of the first secret Jew so identified in the Bible, who, at great risk to her own life, convinced her husband, Babylonian king Ahashuerus, to reverse his decision to massacre the Jews in his kingdom after Prime Minister Haman accused them of treason. Among southwestern Crypto-Jews, the "Feast of Queen Esther" became known as the "Feast of Saint Esther," until recently, when a New Mexico bishop revealed there was no such saint in the Catholic religion and warned that it was part of the Jewish celebration of Purim.

Las Posadas, a nine-day feast when bonfires and candles are lit "to guide the Holy Family looking for shelter", coincides with Hanukkah. It is one of several Christmastime festivals that Crypto-Jews have managed to combine with Jewish customs. A man remembering his own family's secret observances tells how from December sixteenth to the twenty-fourth, his grandmother lit one bonfire for each day: one on the sixteenth, two on the seventeenth, three on the eighteenth, and so on until the ninth day. She told everyone it was a novena to the Child Jesus, but it really symbolized the menorah's eight Hanukkah candles plus the Shammas (the ninth candle, used to light the other eight).

Although pork was prepared only if a family entertained Christian guests, pigs were kept by many Crypto-Jewish families to fool neighbors into believing they raised them for food.

Professor Eduardo Días writes in his book The Crypto-Jews of Portugal how a Christian ritual was assigned a Jewish meaning by a whispered prayer: "'Adonai, my G-d, in my thoughts' (touching the brow); 'Adonai, my G-d, in my lips' (touching the lips); 'Adonai, my G-d, in my heart' (touching the heart). When performed quickly, it is easily taken for the sign of the cross."

Professor David Gitlitz, in his book Secrecy and Deceit: The Lives of Crypto-Jews, describes in detail the many ruses used by them to hide their forbidden activities.

On Yom Kippur, when it was impossible to go out to attend services, secret Jews would go out late at night, often barefooted, to pray in private homes and ask forgiveness of each other.

To keep the fast, one Crypto-Jew was told by his mother to wander around town and refuse all invitations to meals by claiming he had just eaten.

For Sukkot (the Feast of Tabernacles, commemorating the forty years that Jews wandered in the desert after their expulsion from Egypt and erected huts for shelter), the explanation for building a hut out in a field was that bad weather was expected.

One New Mexican man who was caught with matzo hidden under his hat during Passover claimed he was told it would cure his headache.

It is hardly surprising that one practice, established long ago, that persists to this day has also aroused a great deal of controversy and disbelief because

Prologue

it mandates that one male member of each generation of Crypto-Jews be chosen by his family to enter a seminary and be ordained a priest.

Why a priest? As a member of the Catholic clergy he was able to provide a link between their secret world and the Church and give advance warning of any hostile action the local bishops might be planning against their community.

Priests also had legitimate reasons for keeping secrets: the confessional seal gave them that right.

That way, if a Crypto-Jew went to confession, he would always go to his own "family priest." Secrets were passed on that way, and the priest could counsel his people on all spiritual matters in the privacy of the confessional booth.

Although Hebrew texts could be found in some monasteries and better universities, the average Catholic parishioner had access only to the Vulgate. For secret Jews, having a priest in the family meant they could get Hebrew texts for their underground services.

A number of these Jewish priests wielded great influence that helped provide protection for their communities, enabling them to follow their traditional Jewish practices in relative safety.

As might be expected, some Jews forced to submit to baptism and indoctrination fell under the influence of charismatic priests and their conversions were genuine.

Those new Catholics often became the most committed Jew haters and hunters working for the Inquisition. Some of the most famous ones had even been revered leaders of their Jewish communities before they converted and joined the Catholic clergy.

Two of the best known and most infamous were Abner de Burgos, who became Alfonso de Valladolid, and Pablo de Santa María, formerly Rabbi Shlomo de Hallevi, whose claim to fame rests on their often successful efforts to break down Jewish solidarity by subjecting their leaders to public indignities.

Aside from instigating numerous heresy trials, the Church enlisted those high-profile converts to challenge Jewish scholars not only in frequent individual debates but in some well-publicized community spectacles, the infamous "Disputations." The best known were those held in Tortosa, Gerona, and Barcelona.

These public debates pitted the now powerful apostates against their learned and respected Jewish opponents in sometimes months-long and well-staged theological and philosophical pseudobattles claiming to be honest comparisons of the merits of the two religions.

Held in great cathedrals with church prelates as well as royalty in attendance, the general public was eager to witness the debates. Most of them were unaware that the clergy had imposed restrictive and highly slanted rules that ensured that only the Catholic disputants could win.

These lopsided contests were clearly designed to humiliate Jews publicly and shame them and their followers into accepting defeat and conversion.

The Jewish scholars who participated were of course aware that they were being used in a transparent propaganda scheme, but they were forced to go along with the show or risk the Inquisition's vengeance on themselves and their communities. They always lost.

The one exception was Gerona's renowned Kabbalist, Moses Nahmanides (also called Ramban), who, unlike the other Jewish disputants, was granted immunity by King James I and allowed to use all best arguments against his opponent, a converted Jew, now the Dominican monk Pablo Cristiani. After winning the contest and receiving his prize of three hundred solidos (money), the Bishop of Gerona tricked Nahmanides into putting his winning arguments in writing. Now accused of heresy, Nahmanides was promptly banished from Spain and lived out his life in exile in Palestine.[1]

While some of the Jewish converts' resolve to remain true to their heritage buckled under the Church's pressure, for thousands of others baptism meant nothing more than an expedient ruse to escape persecution and death.It provided them with a convenient cover that allowed them to hold on to their

---

1. *The Nahmans of Gerona*, Benjamin Nahman.

lives, their lands, and their positions while they continued to obey their own laws and traditions, maintaining their connection to the G-d of their fathers.

But those who expected that baptism alone would provide them with a secure existence soon found that the opposite was true. As converts they now found their lives trapped under the Church's stringent jurisdiction and control.

Religious zealots working for the Inquisition encouraged the old Catholics to spy on the new converts to make sure they were not backsliding into their heretical practices. They devised clever ways to determine if someone was still guilty of "judaizing" and used devious methods to force secret Jews to unwittingly betray themselves, their friends, and their family members.

Potential informers were given a set of about two hundred to three hundred guidelines to help them identify hidden Jews so they could denounce them. They were told: "If they do any of these practices, you can be sure they are Jews."
The following are some examples:

1. If you see your neighbors wearing fancy, clean clothes on Saturdays, they are Jews.
2. If they clean their homes on Friday night, light candles earlier than usual, and no smoke comes out of their chimneys on those days, they are Jews.
3. If they fast for a whole day until nightfall, they are Jews.
4. If they refer to Queen Esther (who hid her religion and became champion and an inspiration to "Catholics in name only"), they are Jews.
5. If they eat unleavened bread and begin their meal with celery and lettuce during Holy Week, they are Jews.
6. If they say prayers facing a wall, bowing back and forth, they are Jews.
7. If they prepare meat in a special way, draining its blood and cutting away fat and bristle, they are Jews.
8. If they avoid eating pork, rabbits, eels, or any other scaleless fish, they are Jews.
9. If you observe them sitting on the floor, eating eggs and olives, and

throwing morsels of bread into the fire upon the death of a relative, they are Jews.

10. If they name their children after personages in the Old Testament instead of saints and never say: "Glory to the Trinity," they are Jews.

Any convert accused of "fraudulent conversion" by merely pretending allegiance to the Catholic Church risked being tortured until a confession was forced out.

During the three and a half centuries the Inquisition was in operation (1481–1834), thousands of suspects were threatened with death by fire unless they professed the "true faith" and recanted their heretical ways.

Some oral histories collected by descendants describe the following practice: if the accused recanted while tied to the pyre and proved their faith by kissing the cross, they were allowed to die with dry wood, hastening the end, or were "mercifully" garroted before succumbing to the flames. If they refused, they suffered a slow death with green wood. Their relatives were required to bring both kinds of wood to the auto-da-fé (public execution) under threat of sharing the fate of the condemned.

Other oral histories refer to instances when the Church appropriated the "heretic's" property after their execution and awarded one-half to the accuser as a reward. This of course provided Catholic fanatics with a powerful incentive to point their fingers at anyone whose possessions they coveted, whether or not any evidence supported their accusations of heresy. The Inquisitors had all the proper tools to extract the required confessions.

The last known victim to be burned alive, a South American woman, was accused of laying an egg with Hebrew letters on it! Any defense against such "evidence" would have been futile.

In order to escape the Inquisition's torture chambers, all those who chose baptism while continuing to practice their religion in secret had to be particularly clever. They went to great lengths to exhibit extraordinary devotion to the Church to convince every Catholic that they were indeed true converts.

Ironically, no matter how clever, the converts continued to be hounded and harassed by "Old Catholics" who accused them of "sneaking kosher food and lighting candles on Fridays," as well as by unbaptized Jews, who condemned them, saying: "You should have died rather than convert. You are Marranos because you are really Catholics and only pretend to be Jews."

During the last twenty years, an increasing number of contemporary descendants of the medieval Marranos, despite warnings of dire consequences, chose to give up everything that had sustained them within their underground communities.

They broke the strict code of secrecy to escape from their self-imposed restricted, fear-ridden lives by openly proclaiming their Jewishness and allowing "outsiders" to gain a glimpse into the hidden world of their ancestors.

While withholding any specific details of their present-day practices that would identify and thus endanger their families, they provided information about the ruses with which their medieval ancestors had managed to fool the Inquisitors.

They baptized their babies with names of saints, attended church services, participated in the sacraments, and forced their children to attend catechism classes. They kept such forbidden foods as ham and bacon on hand to prove they had rejected Jewish dietary laws and displayed Jesus on the cross, pictures of saints, rosaries, and other evidence of their devotion to the Church in full view to fool a Christian spy.

But in the secrecy of their home they observed traditional practices: they made sure that the meat they ate had been specially slaughtered in respect to the animal, avoided eating pork and shellfish, checked eggs for blood spots, and refused to mix dairy products when serving meat.

They cleaned the house and changed bed linens every Friday, swept all refuse to the center of the room out of respect to the mezuzah, and carefully gathered nail clippings, which were burned.

Burial occurred within twenty-four hours of death, with the body washed and wrapped in a white shroud. They took great care to pass on their Jewish traditions and teachings as best they could from generation to generation.

One Crypto-Jew's ancestors placed a statue of the Madonna by their front door and kissed her foot coming and going, as was the custom at that time. Who would have guessed they had buried a tiny silver mezuzah in the Madonna's foot?

Medieval Marranos were also careful not to reveal to their children that they were Jews until they were old enough to keep a secret. At the age of twelve a grandparent would draw a child aside and disclose the truth: "You are a Jew, and so are we, and you must never tell anyone!"

Often a child would recoil in horror, infected by years of anti-Jewish Church teachings, and run to denounce his or her family to the Inquisition. The interrogators then split up the family, questioned each member separately, told them the others had confessed, breaking down their resistance, and thus achieved their malevolent objectives.

At first those who submitted to baptism under the Inquisition's threats believed that eventually the pressure to conform would abate, as it always had in the past, and they would be able to return to their traditional lifestyle.

But this time the circumstances were different, and the "converts" soon lost all hope that the Church's enforcers would ever allow them to live in Spain as Jews without the specter of persecution at every turn. Remaining hidden under a Christian cover offered the only hope of survival.

After years of practice, caution, and ingenuity, secret Jews soon discovered that despite "conversion," they were unable to escape the fanaticism incited by the Inquisition. Faith was the primary factor determining their fate, and their faith was always suspect.

So, many decided it had become too dangerous to remain in Spain after all. As soon as the New World was discovered, thousands of newly baptized Spanish Jews fled west to wherever they were allowed to settle, certain that crossing the ocean would finally put them beyond the Inquisition's grasp. The opportunity to create a new life, far from the turmoil at home, seemed irresistible to many.

While it is likely that many Marranos who fled to the New World did so as much for practical and economic reasons as to escape religious persecution, by the mid–sixteenth century so many Jewish intellectuals, professionals, and artisans had migrated to the Americas that King Ferdinand became alarmed by the brain drain. He passed a decree forbidding any newly baptized Jews to travel to the New World, but by then it was too late.

In 1571 the Inquisition was ordered to Mexico to control what threatened to be a heretical wildfire out of control. During this renewed period of persecution, tired of fighting what seemed an inescapable tide, many converted Jews gave up the struggle to survive as Jews and quietly became assimilated by blending into their Catholic communities. While some retained a few of their ancestral traditions, it was more out of habit than commitment to their true identities.

But many others were determined to hold on to their religious traditions and practices in secret. They moved north, to what is now the North American Southwest. That is where many of their descendants remain to this day.

Predictably, after enduring years of fear and secrecy and dependent on word-of-mouth transmission of their traditions, far removed from their familial and spiritual roots, the secret Jews gradually changed many of their practices. Eventually some performed ancient rituals, like lighting candles, without knowing why. But others managed to hold on to the essentials and transmit what was most important more or less intact to their descendants.

Only one principle remained constant for all: secrecy and the determination to hide all evidence of their Jewish roots. Since the Inquisition, fear of persecution has been indelibly burned into each Marrano's consciousness to the point of paranoia, passed on from one generation to the next.

Wherever they settled, secret Jews have made a sacred ritual of warning each other to hide their ancestral identities, to remain invisible, to look over their shoulders at all times and be ready to defend themselves against the next inevitable assault.

Through today, those fears are repeatedly justified and reinforced by anti-Jewish uprisings that have occurred with frightening regularity in many countries throughout the world.

Dark visions of entire Jewish communities wiped out with all their synagogues destroyed (as happened in medieval Sevilla and Barcelona) are compulsively kept alive.

Those horror stories and more recent ones describing pogroms in Poland, Russia, and elsewhere throughout Europe are told and retold, with every gory detail minutely spelled out. Even those Jews with only peripheral connections to their roots have never felt safe. They don't feel safe today.

To ensure their survival and maintain their fragile mask, some of the most stringent security measures are, to this day, imposed on their own members by Crypto-Jewish communities: many believe they will be killed if they are ever caught revealing secrets to "outsiders."

Defection is considered treason and once "out," they know they will be disowned, never trusted again by any other secret Jews, especially their own families, or allowed to return.

Even for individual Crypto-Jews who have accidentally discovered evidence of their Jewish blood and have somehow managed to hold on to various fragments of their ancient family traditions alone, without the support of a Crypto-Jewish community to teach them how to live their double lives, secrecy remains the one instinctive constant. For these Jews, hiding their practices from suspicious eyes has become a fine art.

Despite the many difficulties of maintaining their secret lifestyle and constantly coping with perceived dangers, most Crypto-Jews take great pride in their ability to survive, keeping hidden what they value most, fooling the hostile world all around them just as their ancestors did so long ago.

Crypto-Jews sometimes express a certain contempt for mainstream Jews, whose everyday lives, from the Crypto-Jews' point of view, are too easy compared to their own. Would they be willing to endure the Crypto-Jewish lifestyle to safeguard their laws and traditions?

That attitude often makes some secret Jews appear self-righteous and judgmental. It has also kept them strong, prepared for anything that might happen, trained to survive any catastrophe they have been taught to anticipate.

But never has that strength been tested more forcefully, nor the direst predictions proved more tragically prophetic, than in the war that almost exterminated European Jewry fifty years ago, nearly five hundred years after the Spanish Inquisition was established.

Who could have foreseen it would become even more dangerous for Jews to admit their true identities during the Holocaust than during that medieval Jew hunt?

It is ironic that centuries after their persecuted forebears fled north from Spain to settle in the Netherlands, Dutch Crypto-Jews, who had been afraid to reveal their true identities and had remained hidden there for nearly four hundred years, decided in 1920 that it was finally safe to "come out" openly as Jews.

Just twenty years later, most had perished in the Holocaust. As one of the Crypto-Jews warned: "Don't ever tell a Marrano it is safe to come out!"

When Torquemada persuaded Queen Isabella to allow him to cleanse her kingdom of all heresy, he committed himself to ridding Spain of anyone suspected of even the slightest deviation from Catholic dogma. But only if they stubbornly refused to accept the "true faith" did the "heretics" risk death.

Hitler offered Jews no such escape clause: an official baptismal certificate would not stop the Nazis' zeal to exterminate anyone shown to have even the remotest Jewish ancestry. Race, not religion, blood, not faith, were the determining factors for the Nazis, and anyone failing those criteria was a candidate for the gas chamber or any other effective manner of state-mandated murder.

Desperation drove thousands of Jews to circumvent the Nazi racial laws and do what the Marranos had done so long ago: conceal their Jewishness.

They paid outrageous sums of money for fake baptismal certificates and forged passports providing them with Aryan-sounding names. They passed themselves off as Christians until they had escaped safely beyond their persecutors' reach.

Sometimes their masquerade went undetected, and these false documents allowed a few lucky ones to slip through the death net. Others were able to find shelter with courageous Christians who risked their lives to protect them even if they suspected they were sheltering Jews.

Often, as German troops closed in, desperate Jewish parents entrusted their children to Christian families willing to hide them out of an altruistic sense of moral duty or in return for whatever valuables the Jews still owned and offered in payment. Expecting the worst for themselves, Jewish parents hoped this might at least keep their children safe.

Despite the fact that they sometimes spent years away from everything familiar while living in Christian homes, some of the older children clung to memories of their Jewish lives and held on to the hope that their parents would try to come back to claim them.

But as the war dragged on and memories faded, some of the younger children were baptized, raised as Christians, and passed off by the surrogate families as their own.

If the parents survived and were lucky enough to track down their children after searching for them for months, even years, these reunions were often bittersweet. Unable to convince the children that they were Jews and belonged to them, the rightful parents sometimes had to take the families who had saved their children's lives to court to force them to relinquish them.

Pope John Paul recently revealed that after the war, he was instrumental in encouraging Polish Catholics who had sheltered and kept Jewish children to return them to their blood families.

Even if the parents were able to find and reclaim their children (and sometimes they could not), by then it was often too late to restore to the children the Jewish identity of which they were deprived to save their lives. Many Holocaust survivors consider this to be a greater tragedy than their tormented years in the camps.

As far as Crypto-Jews are concerned, they are convinced that history has proved over and over again that no Jew can ever afford to feel safe. They know from their ancestors' painful experiences that hiding under a false cover provides little dependable security, so holding on to their heritage, traditions, and beliefs under a shadow of ever present danger has required tremendous courage and commitment.

That thousands of Crypto-Jews have succeeded in accomplishing this, even in varying degrees of halakhist correctness, is a testimony to their stubborn spiritual dedication. They deserve to be accepted as Jews.

CHAPTER ONE

I first discovered the history of the Marranos as a student at Manhattanville, a Catholic women's college then in New York City. It was run by the Sacred Heart order of nuns, whose convent school in Vienna my mother had attended as a young girl because it was the best school in town.

When I read about those medieval Jews who pretended to be Catholics to escape persecution, I felt an immediate spiritual connection to them, because, like them, I had been hiding my own Jewish identity under a Catholic cover since my father told me when I was eleven years old that it was not safe to be a Jew.

I grew up in Prague, a city renowned for its Jewish culture and rabbinic tradition. It is the home of Franz Kafka, Franz Werfel, and Max Brod, among other famed writers. Prague is also where Rabbi Loew breathed life into a creature he made from clay, called a golem, and ordered him to defend the Prague ghetto Jews in 1579, when they were threatened by a pogrom. Although the golem accomplished the task as ordered, he eventually went out of control and turned violently against his own people, and the rabbi was forced to destroy him. According to the legend, his sandy remains are kept in the roof of the ancient Altneuschul Synagogue, which has been in uninterrupted use since the fourteenth century. Rabbi Loew is buried in the famous cemetery known for its time-tossed tombstones bearing Hebrew inscriptions dating back seven hundred years.

My parents did not consider these legendary, historical, and spiritual treasures of Prague meaningful enough to bring them to my attention. Religion was never discussed. Neither was politics. Other interests and activities took precedence in their value system.

In addition to attending public school (where, among other subjects, I was expected to master Esperanto, the new universal "anti-Babel" language believed by many to be the key to peace and understanding among all the peoples of the world), I had the theater, opera, ballet, and museums as well as art, piano, skating, and swimming lessons to keep me occupied. These activities kept me so busy, I had little time for friends.

From early childhood on, books became my refuge, where I could escape my loneliness and isolation. Books opened up a world for which I hungered without knowing why or what it was: they made me aware of the concept of some kind of supernatural power that controlled everything around me, that connected me to my dreams, fed my fantasies, offered me role models who helped define my sense of justice, taught me what was noble and what was not.

I chose books on ancient mythology, gods and goddesses, about saints and heroes, demons and traitors. The characters in those books became my teachers. Books became my religion. In the midst of the spiritual and emotional vacuum at home, they kept my soul nourished.

In 1938, when Hitler tested his expansionist ambitions by annexing Austria without encountering either local resistance or foreign protest, my parents suddenly announced we would leave Prague and move to Paris. I was afraid to ask why, but I knew from the way they acted that this would not be an ordinary vacation trip.

When they tried to convince my grandmother, Oma Jenny, who lived alone close by, to come with us, she refused.

"Hitler just marched into Vienna—Prague is next," Papa explained.

"What's he going to do with an old lady like me?" she asked, and, despite Mama's pleas, she decided to stay.

We left her behind and settled down in Paris. Oma Jenny later died in the Theresienstadt concentration camp.

I did not know what to make of the cataclysmic events suddenly creating chaos in our lives. I was left to my own devices to provide plausible explanations for the capricious, frightening upheaval over which no one seemed to have any control. There had to be a reason, I reassured myself, even if nothing made any sense to me. Someone, somewhere had to be in charge, had to know what was happening and why. That belief became my link to G-d.

Chapter One

During our eighteen months' stay in France life felt almost normal. I was sent to a boarding school near Versailles, where I learned to speak French, and came home to my parents' tiny hotel apartment on weekends.

Hitler attacked Poland in September 1939, while we were on a short holiday in Normandy. When France and England rose to Poland's defense and declared war, we immediately returned to Paris. Once again our lives were tossed upside down.

Papa, certain this was the beginning of a very explosive situation, disappeared for two weeks, and when he reappeared, he announced we would leave Paris immediately to live in Barcelona.

"At least we will not get shot at in Spain," he explained, because Spaniards were in no position to fight again after a bloody three-year-long civil war that had ended just three months earlier, leaving much of the country in ruins and its people devastated.

I did not know then that Spain's Fascist dictator, Francisco Franco, had just won that war with the help of Hitler and Mussolini, who had used Franco's country as a testing ground for the new, deadly weapons with which they planned to conquer the world.

Not until years later did I discover that during Papa's disappearance, he had made a secret trip to Spain to scout out a safe haven for us. Seeing German soldiers with swastika armbands and SS collar pins helping out with post-civil-war mop-up operations convinced him we had to make some quick changes before leaving France. After announcing we were going to Spain, Papa added he had arranged to have us baptized.

"First we will become Lutherans. Then we will become Catholics, so if anyone asks what we were before, we can say Protestant. . . ."

"Why are we doing this?" I asked.

"Because Hitler is trying to get rid of all Jews."

"Papa, are we Jews?" I asked.

Until that moment, I had no inkling that we were Jews. I also did not understand what it meant to be a Jew, but, remembering what I had read about the saints and heroes who had been ready to die for the truth, I felt

CHAPTER ONE

that what Papa asked us to do was a cowardly lie.

"I don't want to get baptized," I told Papa. "If we are Jews, we should be Jews." He ignored my protest. He was in charge. After all, I was all of eleven years old.

I felt so strongly what we were doing was wrong, I asked to speak alone to the priest conducting the Catholic conversion service. I told him that I did not want to go through with the baptism. After all, did not Joan of Arc refuse to deny her voices no matter what, even if it meant she was going to be burned at the stake?

The priest smiled, put his arm around me, and said: "Do as your father says. Jesus was a Jew. He'll understand."

At that time his words meant little. Moreover, I was certain that by denying who I really was, I would forever forfeit my right to call myself a Jew, whatever that meant. I was convinced G-d would never forgive me.

I did not know then that during the decades before the war, many middle-European Jewish families (including that of former Secretary of State Madeleine Albright, who lived in Prague as a child at the same time as did I) were so convinced that it was dangerous to let their true identities be known, they chose to cut off all connections to their Jewish roots in order to blend smoothly into the Gentile world.

Is it surprising that their traditions, beliefs, everything ethnically and religiously authentic about their past history were all but lost?

Concrete evidence of my own Jewish roots came to light unexpectedly only three years ago when I returned to Prague for a conference the first time after a fifty-six-year absence.

The day before I left, Mama called me.

"I want you should look up my mother's name on the wall inside the Pincas Synagogue . . . ," where the names of all Czechs who perished in concentration camps, including Madeleine Albright's grandparents, were recorded. Mama had never mentioned her mother since Oma Jenny disappeared shortly after Hitler entered Prague in 1938.

Not until that moment.

Chapter One

I found my grandmother's name. Her birth date was correct, but her given name was wrong.

"It's not wrong," Mama said when I told her what I had found, "that's her Hebrew name. . . ."

Even though as a young girl, my mother had been sent to a convent school to be educated by Catholic nuns in Vienna, she knew she was a Jew. Just one generation later, I no longer did.

Throughout my childhood years in Prague my family always celebrated Christmas with candlelit trees and Easter with chocolate bunnies and intricately painted eggs. It was a joyous time with lots of gifts and a break from school. I was unaware of any religious meaning to these festivities.

While my family lived in Spain, I was exposed to religion for the first time. Catholicism as seen through the eyes of a naive, spiritually starved child can be very seductive.

Señora Carron, the elderly Spanish lady whose apartment my family shared in Barcelona for two years, was the mother of a Catalan poet who had fled to the United States when the Fascists won the war. Although like most Spaniards she had been a practicing Catholic before the war, when Franco emerged victorious after unmercifully bombing her city, she stopped attending services.

"G-d is dead," she explained.

Señora Carron had a maid, Pilar, who took me to church with her on Sundays and holy days. My parents did not object.

The pageantry of processions honoring the Blessed Virgin and special saints moving slowly through Barcelona's narrow streets, with children throwing flower petals along their path; the elaborate, mystical ceremonies with the choir singing high mass; the vision of little girls dressed like brides, ready to receive their first communion, with flower wreaths holding fast their white veils; the heady aroma of incense during services, which nearly caused me to faint; and the stained glass windows casting their brilliant shafts of multicolored light into the dusky church nave all wove a magical wonder web around me.

These rituals, with everyone murmuring prayers in unison, filled me with a deep longing. How I wished I could "belong"!

Over and over again I heard at school and during services that Jesus had died for my sins, and for someone feeling as guilty as I for hiding my real identity, Catholicism offered a comforting promise of redemption.

Two years later, when my family finally obtained American visas and sailed for the United States, leaving everything we owned behind for the third time, I had secretly decided to live my life as a Catholic.

I was certain that G-d approved of my decision when, on our arrival in New York, a church refugee organization, intercepting all Catholic arrivals, offered my parents a scholarship enabling me to attend a convent boarding school in New England.

While I was away, my parents settled in an upper Manhattan neighborhood where recent European, mostly Jewish, refugees were clustered.

I loved the three years I spent at Marycliff Academy. I felt safe, peaceful, and contained at the small private school, which was run by an order of French nuns. I learned to speak English and sing Gregorian chants, and everything spiritual I had longed for in Spain was now available to me.

I rarely went home on weekends, but whenever I did, I never missed an opportunity to offer my parents my best arguments why they, too, should convert to "the true faith."

They good-naturedly dismissed my religious zeal as a high fever that would run its course and eventually break. They had no trouble resisting my proselytizing efforts and, as long as I was happy, they did not worry about me.

They would certainly have felt differently had I shared with them my private inner agenda: determined to escape my guilt-ridden past, longing for a peaceful, spiritual existence where all my decisions would be made for me, I was preparing myself to live my life as a nun.

I was sixteen years old in 1944 when I graduated from high school. I moved home to New York after accepting a scholarship to attend Manhattanville College of the Sacred Heart, not far from my parents' apartment, where I hoped to prepare myself for my chosen vocation.

Life in New York proved to be a traumatic change for many reasons.

Living at home while attending college, far from my safe convent school cocoon, I no longer had the support of the caring nuns to sustain me when the real world intruded.

And I no longer had Father Hannegan, Marycliff's chaplain, who had helped me whenever I had difficulty understanding or accepting the strict convent rules. He suffered patiently my early stubborn philosophical challenges to Catholic dogma. He supported my religious vocation, remained my friend even after I confessed my Big Secret to him, and never betrayed my trust.

Commuting to and from college, concentration camp horror stories, no longer vague rumors, glared at me from every newspaper headline, blared at me from every radio broadcast, and my guilt, which I had been able to suppress during my years at Marycliff, reemerged with a vengeance.

Hearing about Hitler's atrocities as his hordes swept across Europe forced me to confront my shame over surviving the Holocaust by fraud while millions of other Jews were bring murdered. I felt I, too, should have died.

As Israel struggled for independence, I wished I could be part of that heroic effort, but I knew I had forever forfeited my right to a Jewish homeland.

Looking for a way to calm my inner turmoil, I began a correspondence with a Maryknoll nun I had met at a religious conference. After several visits to the novitiate I made a commitment to join her missionary order after graduation. I hoped that maybe, if I died a martyr's death in China, I might redeem my sin-scarred soul.

Then something inside me started to change.

I began to question Catholic theological precepts and challenged church rules about such controversial social issues as papal infallibility, the virgin birth, birth control, mixed marriages, and excommunication.

I became increasingly dissatisfied and openly disagreed with the answers the professors, nuns, and priests offered. I soon found myself labeled a troublemaker who was sowing seeds of doubt among my classmates.

But when I heard anti-Semitic jokes expressed by others who had no clue I was born a Jew, I remained silent. This only intensified my shame: I should have objected, but who was I to speak up, to protest, when what I had done (hiding that I was a Jew and escaping my fate by lying) was so much worse?

Then I found out about the Marranos.

While working on a history class research project, I found a book about Spain that briefly mentioned those heretics who had dared to defy the Church, continuing to practice their faith secretly while pretending to be Catholics. I felt an immediate spiritual connection to the secret Jews who had done what I had done yet had not lost their connection with their G-d, my G-d, the G-d of Israel I believed would never forgive me.

Reading about the Marranos gave me a surge of hope. They had managed to hold on to their traditions and beliefs no matter what they had to do to survive, even while hiding that they were Jews. Someday, I promised myself, I would go back to Spain, find some Marranos, talk to them, and learn how to be a Jew from them.

I was nineteen years old when I had to face the fact that my dream would have to remain a dream for a long time, maybe forever. I felt myself slide down a dark spiral into a spiritual no-man's-land: I felt I could no longer remain a Catholic. I also felt I did not have the right to be a Jew.

I was still too ashamed to speak to a rabbi, and there were no Marranos around to rescue me. I felt I belonged nowhere and decided I had to get out of New York, as far away from everything familiar as possible.

I left Manhattanville in my junior year and married a quiet, secular Jew I had recently met, as removed from his spiritual roots as I, who was about to leave town.

We moved to Berkeley, California, where he attended graduate school while I freelanced as a jewelry designer. We had two children, joined a Unitarian congregation (a great place for anyone with an identity problem), and lived a completely unexamined, extraverted life for twelve years devoted to children, work, and little else. I functioned like a well-oiled machine.

Then the machine broke down.

For the next fourteen years I battled depression and survivor guilt demons that taunted me every time I reached out for anything or dared to complain, their voices screaming, "Shut up, you're supposed to be dead!"

Chapter One

I drifted from one black emotional pit into another, from one suicidal panic to the next, while trying to find myself in the psychological maze of analysis.

In 1970, with my children grown and my twenty-two-year-long marriage over, I began to feel I could cope with my inner conflicts at last. I returned to school, earned a master's degree in psychology, and established a private practice in family and art therapy.

I also began slowly, very cautiously, to explore Judaism. I began by reading parts of the Talmud. Then I added books by Moses Maimonedes, Martin Buber, Sholem Alechem, Abraham Heschel, Elie Wiesel, Primo Levy, and other renowned Jewish writers. Often what I read went in one ear and out the other, just one of many manifestations of my persistent ambivalence and resistance.

Eventually I started to occasionally attend services with a newly formed Jewish Renewal congregation that met first in members' living rooms and later, when our membership grew, in a church sanctuary.

Rabbi Ted Falcon, who is also a psychologist, created a welcoming, unthreatening, and open atmosphere that, in addition to all the halakhicly correct rituals for Shabbat and traditional holy days, also included such New Age modalities as chanting and meditation.

His sermons were always stimulating and thought provoking; the choir, which quickly attracted some remarkable voices, was uplifting; and the group discussions during frequent retreats allowed me to express my questions and feelings of discomfort without fear of being ostracized.

Although none of these observances and rituals ever evoked the same feelings of rapture and awe as the church services I remember attending as a child in Spain, in time I felt comfortable enough to formally join the congregation as a member.

In 1988 I finally felt ready to look for the Jewish roots I had lost as a child. That four-year journey of discovery is chronicled in my first book, *The Mezuzah in the Madonna's Foot, Marranos and Other Secret Jews: A Woman Discovers Her Spiritual Heritage*. It was on that search I encountered my first Crypto-Jews and slowly began groping my way back to where I felt I belonged.

Chapter Two

Several years ago, while still struggling to come to terms with my own denial of my Jewish identity, I met "Matthew," a Catholic priest who had spent many years as the assistant to a bishop in a major U.S. city. He was also a secret Jew.

Five days a week he performed his customary priestly duties: saying mass, listening to confessions, officiating at baptisms, weddings, and funerals.

On weekends he joined the local Orthodox Jewish community, where he regularly attended services for Shabbat and other holy day observances. His dual identity was well known to its members, who seemed to accept his status as a secret Jew.

Matthew lived in constant fear of being found out. When he began to notice subtle but significant changes in the bishop's attitude toward him (such as assigning him special duties on Fridays and Saturdays), he became convinced he was about to be unmasked.

Although he knew what the consequences would be, he decided to leave the Church, abandon his secret life, and live openly as a member of the community of Orthodox Jews, who by then had come to know him as the "Jewish priest" who had worshiped with them for years.

When Matthew told the rabbi about his decision and asked to be accepted officially as a member, he was told: "You realize, of course, you must convert if you want to be one of us."

"Convert from what, to what?" he cried. "I have always been a Jew—my ancestors were burned at the stake because they were Jews!"

The rabbi's decision remained firm. Overnight Matthew went from being accepted as a "secret Jew" to a suspected "phony priest."

Suddenly no one trusted him. No one offered him a job commensurate with his education or expertise. He felt deeply hurt and betrayed by

Chapter Two

this rejection by his own people.

Matthew and I met during this traumatic time, when he was struggling to cope with his new life, suddenly cut off from the power and financial security he once had as a priest.

"When a priest leaves the Church, there is nothing he can take with him. No severance pay, no references to help him survive. He has lost his community, his family, his support system. And his credibility."

At first Matthew was reluctant to talk about himself, but once he knew about my own background, he seemed to let down his guard. In time he became remarkably open about certain parts of the Marrano experience, willing to help me with details I would never have found in books.

Because he had researched his own family history in Vatican archives, he was able to offer very personal details. It was his own medieval ancestors who had buried a mezuzah in the foot of the Madonna statue by their front door to fool the Inquisition's spies.

Long before information about his people had become public knowledge, it was he who told me about the thousands of contemporary Crypto-Jews who live in the American Southwest. And it was he who revealed their centuries-old tradition of designating one male member of each generation to become a priest.

After I told him I was writing a book, we spent many hours talking about his life and his people's history. Nevertheless, he remained cautious: he never answered his phone until he heard my voice on his answering machine. He only gave me a PO box number so I never knew where he lived. But he occasionally accepted invitations to come to my home, when he was in town. I felt he eventually achieved a measure of trust and comfort with me.

But it was an effort for Matthew to keep from sinking into depression. For a long time he worked at temporary jobs far below his capacity. Then he was finally offered a prestigious executive position with a Sephardic community of a large city, for which he was eminently qualified.

He was overjoyed and ready to accept the job until he read the small print of his contract.

It stated that in order to be accepted for employment, he would have to reveal everything about his own past, as well as that of his family, as if to verify his claim as a bona fide Marrano. He was expected to provide everyone's real name and origin, their course of immigration, proof of their matrilineal correctness, rabbinical records, etc.

Matthew was devastated. If his qualifications were as satisfactory as they assured him they were, he asked, why did they need all this information about his ancestral background? Were they planning to exhibit him as a living anachronism, like a freak in a sideshow?

Matthew assured them he would have no problem corroborating all his claims but explained that to do so would mean betraying his family.

When he told me the news, I shared his outrage.

"Don't they know we are a secret society?" he stormed. "Revealing these facts about my family goes against my Marrano soul. . . ."

After agonizing over his decision for weeks, he turned down the job. The letter he wrote explaining his reasons poignantly describes the life of a present-day Crypto-Jewish priest.

"Marranos, by definition, are secret Jews. The main reason we have survived all these centuries is because we have refused to come out into the open. This, of course, has made us suspect in the eyes of both Catholics and Jews. With this suspicion we have had to live.

"I see it as a great honor to be offered this position. However, revealing my Marrano background in depth, exposing my family's customs to the scrutiny of others, even though they might be well-intentioned individuals and sincerely interested, is something I am unwilling to do. I cannot be the one to expose my ancestors or in any way unmask my living relatives.

"There might be Gentiles today who cannot understand the preoccupation of Jews with the Holocaust. Such persons do not understand how the Holocaust colors much of modern Judaism, like fallout after a nuclear blast, which lingers for centuries in the atmosphere.

"So, too, not many Jews can fathom the loneliness of a Marrano when, even within our own family, we can never be sure whether someone will betray us out of fear, greed, envy, hatred, or stupidity.

"My family and I have been scrutinized, interviewed, investigated, examined, and studied by individuals and committees, by priests, by rabbis, by scholars, and by neighbors for centuries.

"Those of us whom G-d gave the gift of clever speech were able to sidestep questions, talk our way out of tight spots. Those of us who made a false step perished.

"Somehow the inquiry you propose still echoes to me of the Inquisition. I may be guilty until proven innocent, or innocent until proven guilty. . . . Or I might be authentic until proven inauthentic, or inauthentic until proven authentic. . . . In any case, there will be questions and more questions. And then there will be a decision. About me. About my family. That is too high a price for me to pay.

"If your community wants my involvement with your project, good. I have no wife or children to distract me from my task. But my Marranism, other than a passing fact about me, should not play a role in the performance of my duties or affect my relationship to anyone.

"I know your stated goal is to simply verify the facts about my past and then to go on. But I am telling you, I am very experienced as to the reaction of Jews as well as Gentiles to Marranism. The skepticism never ends but only spreads, until ever more proof is demanded.

"When scientists want to find out what makes a bird live, if they dissect the bird, they may find out all about it, but in doing so they have killed it. It is the same with a Marrano. In satisfying another's curiosity in verifying his reality, the Marrano has been put through the Inquisition. AGAIN! This is our weakness, but it must be dealt with.

"I want no more inquisitions. I have been through Roman Catholic seminary board inquisitions before bishops, priests, fellow seminarians, roommates, and coworkers. I have been through diocesan inquisitions before the Bishop's Council. I will not sit through any more inquisitions, even Jewish ones.

"ESPECIALLY JEWISH ONES!"

Chapter Two

"Jews, above all, should respect my sentiments."[1]

For a long time Matthew struggled along, supporting himself with short-term jobs for which he was vastly overqualified. But, convinced he would never find a job befitting his education and experience without references unless he revealed all about his own past and that of his family, which would have jeopardized their cover, he eventually went underground again and once more hid his Jewish identity under a priestly cover, but as a rogue cleric, unsanctioned by the official Catholic Church.

Once, when a trip brought me close to where he was living, we met and had dinner at a restaurant near his church. It was a weekend night, and the dining room was packed. Matthew and I were sitting in a booth, deep in conversation, when a young boy approached our table.

"Father, how nice to see you!"

They shook hands and had a little conversation. Then the boy asked: "Father, will you bless me?"

Matthew got up as the boy knelt beside our booth, in full view of everyone around us, and made a sign of the cross over his head, mumbling something in Latin. The boy rose, thanked his priest, then shook his hand before walking off.

Matthew turned back to me, sat down, and continued our conversation exactly where we left off without blinking or missing a beat . . . while I held my breath, amazed at his chameleonlike ability to switch roles from one second to the next. He was clearly a master of the art of camouflage.

Disillusioned and growing increasingly bitter, Matthew eventually made it clear he was now willing to offer only the kind of generic information that would in no way jeopardize or reveal too much about the Crypto-Jews' lifestyle.

He still derived a certain perverse pride in his complex heritage and was determined to defend its secretiveness at every turn.

"If we wanted the world to know all about us, we would not live this

---

1. First quoted in *The Mezuzah in the Madonna's Foot*

secret life. We hide because we want to be invisible. Probe too much and we'll lie . . . or disappear."

Despite everything, Matthew has remained deeply Jewish. He considers himself Orthodox, keeps kosher, and knows more about Jewish history, traditions, and practices as well as those of the Catholic Church than anyone I have ever met. At one point he agreed to give me lessons in how to be "a real Jew" once I had completed my book.

As I turned to him for more and more details about the Crypto-Jewish lifestyle, I sensed he was getting tired of all the questions. I knew it was time to back off, but my editor kept pushing me to get Matthew to elaborate on some facts about his ancestors' life under the Inquisition that he had volunteered but on which he was reluctant to offer any specific additional details.

Although I instinctively knew that I was about to cross an invisible line, I allowed myself to be persuaded to press for "just this one last missing piece of the puzzle."

I called Matthew. When I told him what my editor wanted to know, there was a long silence.

"Matthew, are you there?" I asked, thinking we had lost our phone connection.

More silence. Then there came a sound I can only describe as something like a primordial animal scream/moan.

"Enough, enough . . . I cannot go back there anymore. . . . Don't they understand? It's not over! It will never be over! Nothing has changed!"

Before I could assure him he did not have to say another word, he hung up. For many months he refused to answer or return my calls.

I was certain our connection was irreparably broken, but the day my book was published, with an abridged chapter about Matthew, I made one last try to contact him. I could hardly believe it when I heard him answer the phone. He did not offer an apology or explanation for his disappearance, and I did not ask for any. I had learned my lesson.

However, things were never quite the same as before. He seemed much more guarded, much more leery of any intrusion into his life. I could hardly blame him.

Although I believed the essence of what Matthew had shared with me during the months we worked together, most of which was later corroborated by other researchers' investigations into the Marrano experience, I knew from the start there was no way I could verify or prove anything specific he told me. After all, he had made it clear again and again that Crypto-Jews were able to survive years of persecution and surveillance only if they mastered the art of weaving a clever web of misinformation about themselves to confuse and throw the pursuers off their track.

Along the way, Matthew had revealed some parts about his life that were so hard to believe, I chose not to include them in my book. Among them were claims of participating in some clandestine negotiations involving our government. He even named rather prominent persons who were part of these affairs. It all sounded too much like something out of a James Bond spy mystery to be taken seriously.

Because I knew that Crypto-Jews are taught to spin deceptive webs whenever they feel threatened, I simply ignored what seemed suspect. Besides, I was much more interested in the psychological atmosphere created by the constant fear with which Crypto-Jews lived their everyday lives, and how they coped with it, than in improbable heroics and unverifiable statistics.

Some months after my book was published, I was approached by a young, award-winning playwright, well known in Jewish circles, who expressed an interest in doing a play about Matthew's life.

Although she did not offer to option my book, she assured me I would be solidly involved in the project and asked if I could arrange a meeting with Matthew.

"I just want the priest's story," she said. "It'll make a terrific play!"

"Forget it!" I told her. "Matthew will never agree to it." I nevertheless promised to relay her offer to him.

Matthew's response was totally unexpected: he agreed to a meeting.

I arranged for the three of us to meet. For over an hour I sat silently watching him casually expose various facets of his life, including many details he had never shared with me.

I was puzzled by Matthew's openness. How come he was so candid with someone he had never met before? I saw none of the hesitancy and discomfort I had learned to expect in my dealings with him.

At one point he described his painful response to a particularly virulent anti-Semitic lecture by a priest when he was a young seminarian.

"I felt such guilt over my silence, I snuck into the chapel after everyone went to sleep, prostrated myself before the cross, and begged Rabbi Jesus to forgive me."

Remembering my own shame and anguish at keeping silent when I heard others, who had no clue about my own true identity, making derogatory remarks about Jews, I reached out to touch Matthew's hand to express my sympathy.

The playwright's breathless response was: "Ah, perfect! That's the end of act one!"

I watched Matthew flinch ever so slightly, but he revealed no other reaction to her blatant insensitivity as he continued.

Retelling some of the stories he had told me that I had dismissed as fanciful fabrications, he now opened a briefcase he had brought along and produced photo after corroborating photo of himself, in priest's garb, in the company of various well-recognizable persons in high U.S. and foreign government positions, with whom he had claimed to have worked on his various capers!

He had never shown me these photos. What in the world possessed him to reveal so much to this complete stranger?

The writer could hardly contain her excitement at the prospect of dramatizing Matthew's story. She tried to get him to give her his address and phone number so she could consult with him directly as she proceeded with the project, but he refused.

"Call Trudi. She will pass on all your questions to me."

With her enthusiasm only slightly dampened, the playwright spouted promises and predictions of success and left.

"What were you thinking, giving her all this information about you?" I asked as soon as she was gone. "Aren't you afraid she'll blow your cover?"

"How will she prove anything?" Matthew replied with a sly smile. "She doesn't know who I really am or how to reach me. I'm not listed anywhere."

"How do you feel about working with her?"

"What makes you think I plan to work with her?"

"So what was this all about? If you don't intend to work with her, why did you tell her so much about you?"

"I wanted to lure her into my net, to watch her squirm with greed. I wanted to give her just a little taste, to whet her appetite so I could give her the finger when she was hooked and begged for more. . . . Besides, nothing will come of this. You don't really believe she was planning to keep us both involved in her project, do you?"

"What do you mean? She can't do this alone. She needs us. She said we would all work together—"

Matthew interrupted.

"Trudi, let me draw you a picture. She thinks I'm upstairs on the second floor of a house. She's downstairs, trying to get to me. You are the ladder. Once she is upstairs, she'll kick away the ladder. . . ."

When I looked skeptical and tried to offer an argument for at least giving her the benefit of the doubt, he added:

"Forget it. You can't be a priest doing counseling, listening to confessions, dealing with everyone from ordinary parishioners to powerful politicians for eleven years without becoming expert at reading people. . . . You learn to spot the phonies, the liars, the spinners."

Matthew proved to be right. When the writer realized that rather than getting rid of me, she now had to depend on me for her connection to Matthew, she tried to convince me to exclude him from the project. The contract she offered never mentioned his name.

When I called her attention to the oversight, she laughed. Didn't I realize how much money would be involved if the play were ever made into a film? Did I really want to share that with Matthew? After all, she cajoled, "we" don't really need him: "we" already knew enough about him!

When I insisted that Matthew would have to remain part of the project because after all, it was HIS story, she abruptly withdrew all offers.

Although Matthew and I stayed in touch for some time after that incident, he became increasingly bitter and disillusioned and ultimately cut off all contact.

I continued my research and, four years later, in the spring of 1997, I was approached by two different film producers who had read my book and were fascinated with the stories about the secret Jews. Each asked if I would be interested in developing a fictional film story with a contemporary Crypto-Jewish theme. And both asked that the main character be a Jewish priest!

I had never written fiction before, but I was sufficiently intrigued by the prospect of creating a story and inventing characters that I agreed to give it a try.

I knew I could not possibly be involved in two identical projects simultaneously. So, although one of the producers was already well established with an impressive reputation, I opted to work with the one who had approached me first: a young Jewish filmmaker, who had only recently set up his own production company after a long apprenticeship with a studio renowned for its successful independent films.

He had also spent years on his own spiritual journey. We hit it off immediately. I felt I could trust his integrity and agreed we would work well together.

Although the story would be fictitious, I was glad my years of research would give my work a solid factual grounding. I was determined to make it so real that the audience would feel immersed in the Crypto-Jewish world. I was hoping that this might in some small way break down some of the barriers of ignorance and prejudice that have kept secret Jews locked in their medieval spiritual prison.

I decided to set my story in present-day New Mexico, where the largest number of Crypto-Jewish families (estimated at fifteen hundred) is known to live.

What I did not anticipate was the emotional impact of becoming so involved in the lives of my fictional characters as they struggled with the problems their real-life counterparts face daily.

Presenting all aspects of the controversy surrounding secret Jews forced me to confront my conflicted feelings about Crypto-Jews in general and Crypto-Jewish priests in particular.

One part of me felt a deep kinship with them, understood their fears, and was supportive of their right to keep their ancestors' traditions alive. I was sympathetic and respectful of their need to hide and do whatever they had to do in order to survive.

Another part of me wondered if those traditions had perhaps outlived their purpose, meaning, and intent. Had the Crypto-Jews' lifestyle become an anachronism? Had the time come to search for a different approach to ensure their survival, to find a healing reconnection between secret Jews and their mainstream brothers in order to live their true identities openly at last?

How would their community respond if an outsider like myself dared to challenge their time-tested tradition of banishing one of their sons into the bosom of the Church as a priest?

After all, who was I to question the morality of condemning the chosen one to a solitary, conflicted, and severely restricted double life, without a family of his own, a life even more difficult and dangerous than their own?

Those concerns troubled me for a long time.

It took a year to create the framework for the film story. I finally felt ready to submit the first draft to my producer on June 16, 1998. Before sending it off, I called him.

"I don't know about this project," I admitted. "Who in the world is going to believe that anyone would choose to live like this, here, today . . . accept that these people actually exist?"

"Don't worry," he reassured me. "Remember, we're talking about New Mexico. They have UFOs. Why not Crypto-Jews?"

He was joking, of course, but I had serious doubts about the viability of

Chapter Two

our project. After all, the existence of Crypto-Jews was still either mostly unknown or considered too strange to accept even by many well-informed Jews. How could we expect the general public to be less skeptical?

I also had concerns about how the Crypto-Jewish community would react to a film revealing many aspects of their lives, even though it depicted only fictionalized situations and characters.

For years they had trusted me with their secrets. I had never betrayed their confidences, never exposed their identities. Would they now feel I was exploiting them?

Would they approve of my reasons for giving details about their traditions, using their history to justify their secrecy and deceptions on the one hand, while hoping it might help pave the way to their acceptance by mainstream Jews and perhaps even make continuing to live a lie unnecessary?

When my film story was nearly completed, my producer offered to send me to Writers Boot Camp to take their screen-writing course.

"No one knows the subject, the nuances of the Crypto-Jews' lives better than you. You write the script."

In order to provide my film with the most authentic, personal details of Crypto-Jewish everyday life, I posted a Web page on the Internet the day before I sent off my film story, detailing my continuing research and asking for specific information about present-day Crypto-Jewish practices, religious rituals, customs, belief systems, and recipes, with a promise to keep any identifying data confidential. I was planning to weave those details into the script's background pattern.

When I sent off my manuscript, I had no idea how eerily it would echo the drama in the life of the Crypto-Jewish priest who was about to appear in my life.

CHAPTER THREE

JUNE 1998

Two days after I sent off my film story, I received the first e-mail letter from "Simon." He had found my Web page on the Internet the day I posted it and felt compelled to write.

With our correspondence ongoing as I write, I now have more than seventy-five letters from him. For security reasons I automatically erase all our letters but keep the original print copies in a locked metal safe, in the event their authenticity should ever be challenged.

As you read our letters, you will find that Simon does not immediately respond to many of my questions. At first I was so glad he was willing to share information with me that I did not dare mention what seemed to be his apparent evasiveness.

When I finally expressed my frustration at having had to repeat my questions again and again, he apologized and explained that writing to me is very risky: although he has a private computer on which he receives e-mail, like me, he erases my letters immediately. But unlike me, he does not dare to make print copies, so he sometimes forgets some of my questions by the time he gets to the safety of a public computer place to reply to me.

Although Simon's English is quite good, his syntax is sometimes a bit convoluted and his spelling is phonetic, like his native Spanish, so I am taking the liberty to do some minor editing merely in the service of better comprehension and to delete all identifying names and places.

I will also skip over several letters of minimal interest, occasionally condense a number of others, or edit out what seems irrelevant or repetitive. Some of the letters are quoted together but out of sequence, in the interest of subject continuity. Despite these minor changes, our correspondence will appear with its most important content intact.

Chapter Three

Thursday, June 18, 1998
Dear Mrs. Alexy,

My name is Simon _____

   I am a Spaniard, but I was born and live in Latin America. Four years ago I read your book, The Mezuzah in the Madonna's Foot, and I have to be honest, it really shook me. It describes my family.

   I am a member of a large secret Jew community here in _____. This community is conformed of more than three hundred people.

   Believe it or not, we have our own secret temples, our own rabbi, we try to adapt our practices to modern Judaism, we have been married within our own people, "con los nuestros," for years, but we live as Catholics, taking part in many other Catholic activities, trying to live in peace, . . . and always with fear.

   My family arrived in _____ in the XVIIth century, they settled down in the province of _____ , and, in order to be accepted in this area they changed their Jewish name to _____ , a Spanish name not very common in this area, so they will remember always their Jewish roots.

   Many kosher customs were passed from generation to generation as simple family rules, like not eating pork because it is not healthy, avoiding going to funerals, putting rocks on tombstones instead of flowers, and never give offerings in church.

   My grandfather taught me to use the tallith and tefillin in the traditional way. Secret Jews are a reality. We are still living in fear.

   As a scholar, I believe it is your mission to not only investigate and do research of us to show the world, but to provide new ways in which the Jewish people will accept us again.

   We never rejected Judaism. In many cases it has been a miracle to keep alive the traditions of our fathers. Can you imagine how it feels to know you are Jewish and feeling as a stranger in a synagogue???

   Many people here in Latin America read your book and since then it has been necessary for us to take precautions, because the Catholic authorities here

*are always looking for conversos, even in indirect ways, but they are. As they
did five hundred years ago. However, as a result of your book, many people
understand the consequences of religious fanaticism. The Inquisition was one
of this expression.*

Thanks a lot,
Simon_____

▼▼▼

I stared at the monitor in disbelief. Who was this person? What led him to
find me now, just when I was filled with doubt and looking for guidance in
my search for answers?

There was no way of knowing the letter's point of origin from the e-
mail address. Although he identified a country south of the U.S. border, the
e-mail could have been sent from anywhere in the world, even right around
the corner. Yet here was someone who claimed to be a Crypto-Jew writing
to encourage me to go ahead with my project!

My gut response was that the letter was genuine, but I was afraid to rely
solely on my own assessment. Was it a matter of wishful thinking?

As I reread the letter again and again, I had to ask myself: How objective
was I? Could this possibly be a fraud? And what would be this man's motive
for writing it if it were a hoax?

I let several reliable colleagues read Simon's letter with all names and
locations blacked out. The consensus reached was that it appeared to be
authentic.

Whatever concerns I had almost vanished.

I answered immediately.

Chapter Three

Friday, June 19, 1998
Dear Simon,

Thank you so much for your letter. Your information is most important, and I would appreciate you letting me know any additional details of your customs and rituals for my continuing research.

How did your rabbi become a rabbi?

Where was he educated?

What sorts of rituals does he perform?

Do your men get circumcised?

What kinds of traditional foods do you eat?

Please keep me informed of any details of your everyday life you might be able to provide.

How do you celebrate your holidays, and what do you do when Catholics celebrate theirs?

Do you speak Ladino?

I am really excited you made contact with me. I am most grateful.

Please respond.

Trudi Alexy

It took another day for the real meaning of what had happened to sink in. If authentic, Simon's letter was a miracle! Here was a secret Jew who, like Matthew, appeared to be living a hidden life as a priest but, unlike Matthew, did so within a Crypto-Jewish community.

How fortunate to finally have the opportunity to carry on a dialogue with someone who might be able to provide me with a window into his present-day world, from the inside out!

I felt this man spoke from his heart, pleading for understanding, for acceptance, for an end to his people's exile.

I wrote again, without waiting for Simon to respond.

CHAPTER THREE

Sunday, June 21, 1998
Dear Simon,

I was so excited to get your letter that I felt I had to respond immediately. Only after I sent off my e-mail to you and reread again and again what you wrote did your words really hit home.

Thank you again for sharing your story with me.

Shalom,
Trudi

▼▼▼

Two days later another letter appeared.

Tuesday, June 23, 1998
Dear Trudi,

To be honest, I never expected to get an answer from you.

I am glad you can understand how I feel and how many, many other people feel. Sure, you can count on me for any information that might help you with your research. However, I do only ask for two conditions:

1. That you maintain in secret my identity.

2. That in every paper, or essay, or book that you might write in the future, I would like you to emphasize not only that secret Jews exist, but most of all [show] the tremendous problem that we face now: persecution and rejection by the Jewish people. As a scholar, I believe you can do a lot about that.

I hope that this will be the beginning of a good friendship. I have decided to come out of secretivity [sic] and get in touch with you because the life of secret Jews is not very pleasant. Our main problem is to live hidden in times of no Inquisition.

Thanks, and I hope for your prompt answer.

Don't worry if you don't hear from me for a few days. I will be traveling to _____, so don't worry if you don't right away get an answer for your letter.

Keep in touch.
Simon

▼▼▼

Even though it all seemed quite surreal, I was beginning to feel that perhaps this time I was going to get some answers directly from a source that no one, to my knowledge, had ever tapped before in quite the same way: not set in the past, but today. I allowed myself a glimmer of hope.

Tuesday, June 23, 1998
Dear Simon,

    Thank you for responding so quickly.
    I am so grateful you are willing to help me with my research, and of course, I will keep your identity secret, as I did with Matthew.
    There are so many things I don't know, but we will go very slowly so you can begin to feel comfortable with the way I work.
    I, too, look forward to developing a friendly relationship based on mutual trust.
    Cold "facts" about secret Jews are getting better and better known. What is not known is the spiritual atmosphere within the Crypto-Jewish community.
    What sustains you? What sort of persecution are you afraid of, and what kind of rejection have you experienced?
    I sense that you fear mainstream Jews' response to you more than that of the Christians. Is this so?
    What do you think will happen if any of them find out about you? Do you expect a simple rejection or, worse, a humiliating exposure as an impostor or liar, "not really a Jew," or a "shunning," like among the Mormons?
    Are you afraid someone might actually physically hurt you or your family?
    What keeps you holding on to the secrecy even though there is no Inquisition? Is it

a tradition you are proud of, keeping the Jewish laws in spite of the potential danger?

As you can see, the researcher in me has a million questions! If this is too much, let me know and I will back off and be patient. I will appreciate every small piece of the puzzle you are willing to share.

To do a good, authentic job with what I write, I have to truly understand the feelings, the essence behind the secret Jewish traditions, what has kept them sacred and alive for so many centuries.

Enough for now! Have a good trip.

Shalom,
Trudi

▼▼▼

Thursday, June 25, 1998
Dear Trudi,

Well, I can see you have a hard task for your research, but I hope to be helpful.

You ask me about the spiritual atmosphere in the Crypto-Jewish community.

First of all, there are main differences inside the Crypto-Jewish community (if a community exists): one wing considers Christianism [sic] only as a mask, another wing believes in Christianish [sic], and many others know about their Jewish origins but have no consciousness about it.

In my case, I was raised as a Catholic . . . later, at the age of twelve, I was told what I was. I entered a Catholic theological seminary at age fifteen, knowing of course what I was.

Every morning I had to pray "Salve Maria, benedicta tu di tutti donna" [Hail Mary, blessed are you among all women], and in my heart I was crying "Baruch Ata Adonai Melech Ha Olam . . ." [Blessed be our G-d, the one G-d, King of the universe] and in my most secret moments, alone and

Chapter Three

afraid in the darkness of my tallith, I was able to pray "Shema Israel,
Adonai Eloheynu Adonoi Ehad . . . Ehad . . ." [Hear O Israel, Lord our
G-d, the Lord is one, our one and only G-d].

I have to face it: I consider myself a Jew, yet I have to pray in secret!
Why??? The Judaism I practice is just and the essence of normal Judaism.
Still, every time I go to a synagogue, I have to wear one of the paper kippas
and sit on the visitor side! Why???

When do you keep things secret? Only when you are not sure, or you
think what you are doing is wrong. But many secret Jews are proud of their
ancient traditions, traditions that are hard to understand.

Six months ago one of my best friends decided to come out of secretivity.
He went to the local rabbi to explain his case. The rabbi, a Sephardic Jew,
understood him, but the rest of the committee, many of them Ashkenazim,
asked my friend to convert.

He agreed. I went to his Bar Mitzvah, as an invited guest (nobody knew
I was a secret Jew), and I had to see how my friend had to go through the
ritual purification, was treated like a Gentile! I asked myself, he had to
convert from what?

Many other Jews have to suffer this humiliation, so, after they "convert"
to Judaism, they don't ever speak of their Marrano identity, they pass
themselves off as normal (converted) Gentiles.

Why do they do this? you might ask. Trudi, this is the reality: you get
tired of living in secret, you get tired of always checking behind your back,
you get tired of fearing rejection from your own family!!!!

In many Marrano families only one of the sons is chosen to carry the
tradition. The rest of the family, sometimes even the parents, never discover
their Jewish identity.

See, in my case, my parents are Catholics. So are my brothers. My
grandfather chose me and explained to me what I am. My uncle was chosen
by him (before me) to carry the family tradition. And that's it! No more
Marranos in my family!

Right now it is hard to keep this secret even in one's own family. . . .

Many secret Jews here in Latin America are converting to Protestantism because the Evangelical Church is very friendly to everything Jewish.

As you know, it is very common for many Evangelicals to have menorahs and shofars in their homes, so many secret Jews have a chance to wear a new mask . . . and they can avoid the typical questions: "Why do you have this? Why do you have that? Are you Jewish?"

I hope this letter is not too long.

I'll talk to you in two weeks when I get back from my trip.

Take care.

Simon

▼▼▼

I quickly wrote to apologize for asking so many new questions, hoping to get an answer prior to his departure, but it was three weeks before I got another letter.

Wednesday, July 15, 1998

Hi, there!

Well, I am back from _____. Everything went well, thank G-d.

Don't worry about the many questions. It is my pleasure to help. Just let me go one by one.

About Crypto-Jewish observances, there is a kind of principle to be set: you want to celebrate without celebrating.

There is a main difference between our religious methodology and the mainstream way of practicing Judaism, because of our secretivity.

After living many years in secret and losing the relationship with other Jewish people, practices do change.

And, again there is the matter of secretivity: you don't want to celebrate a Shabbat and let anyone know what you are doing.

The whole thing of being a Marrano is to live two lives and purposely

Chapter Three

not let anyone know about your roots.

Because of this, the observances, the alimentary traditions, the religious methodology are reduced to their main essence.

Take the Shabbat, for example. What is the main biblical and Talmudic principle about the Shabbat? Keeping some special ritual, singing some special songs, eating bread and drinking wine? Or is it to rest, and keeping that day holy and separate for G-d?

So, as a Marrano, instead of going to the synagogue on Friday, or celebrating a Shabbat family dinner, you take time to rest, to pray, to stay home to celebrate the feast. . . .

You don't go to movies as all your friends will do, you don't go to parties or any social gathering on Friday, you keep the essence of the day: resting and keeping the day for G-d.

Basically, the secret Jewish services are not held in Hebrew because it is a language that not everyone in the community understands.

The same problem arises with Ladino. Only the ancient people in the community, the "elders," are the ones that keep this tradition alive.

What about Yom Kippur and other feasts? The way of observing may be different from people to people, but for centuries secret Jews have been doing the same thing: the main key is not to keep the ritual but to keep the spiritual purpose!!

That's the life of a Marrano.

Can you understand why many of us have decided to come into the light? If you ask for some rituals and observances among us, few can be seen.

Well, take care.

I'll keep in touch.
Simon

▼▼▼

There was something about the way he began his letter that made me feel uneasy. But I was reluctant to ask if anything had happened on his trip, afraid it would appear too invasive.

While I was touched by Simon's simple, pure spirituality, I was even more affected by his conflicted feelings about his dual life: commitment and pride in his ancient heritage, yes, but a barely concealed anger and resentment at having to live in the dark.

I wanted to ask him, "What keeps you there? Why don't you come out into the light, as some others have done?" but felt I had no right to be so confrontational, so soon.

At this point I also wondered if he was in fact a priest, as I first assumed. He mentioned earlier that he had been "sent to a theological seminary" when he was fifteen, but he never spelled out that he had actually become a priest.

Did he complete his studies there?

Was he ever ordained?

Is he a member of the clergy now?

So many unanswered questions!

I decided to risk asking him to elaborate on some of his vague responses but deemed it prudent to hold back some of my personal concerns.

Wednesday, July 15, 1998
Dear Simon,

Glad things went well in_____, and you had a safe return.

Each time you write, I get a better sense of what it is like to live a Marrano life. I wish I could be a fly on the wall and experience it as you live it, with all the conflicting feelings but from a safe distance, realizing I don't have the centuries of tradition to really make it mine. So, I depend on your words to get me as close as I can ever get.

Here come some more questions.

When you speak of you and your uncle being chosen "to carry the family tradition," do you mean that you were told by your grandfather that you are secret Jews and learning how to perform the Crypto-Jewish practices? Or is

Chapter Three

it that you were sent to the seminary to become priests? Or both? I hope you can clarify this.

With your parents and the rest of the family practicing Catholics, where and how did you learn to be a Jew? Did your grandfather teach you everything?

What was it like to live in a Catholic seminary? How did you manage to hide your Jewishness from everybody?

Please let me know if I ask too may questions or if am becoming too personal. Write soon.

Shalom,
Trudi

▼▼▼

When I did not hear anything from Simon for nearly a week, I got worried. Did I go too far? Did I blow him away already?

I remembered how painful it was when Matthew abruptly disappeared for nearly two years while I was in the middle of writing my first book, unable and unwilling to deal with my questions.

I knew there was no way to predict how Simon would react to my inquiries, no matter how willing he appeared to be now. After all, I had not really begun to get into the nitty-gritty of my exploration into the Crypto-Jewish soul.

Realizing this, I knew I had to proceed very cautiously.

Tuesday, July 21, 1998
Dear Simon,

Did I offend you by something I said? Perhaps you misunderstood when I said I wanted to be a fly on the wall to experience everything myself. That did not mean I wanted to spy on you! I just sometimes wished I could get closer, to feel what it was like to belong. . . .

It makes me sad that things are so hard for secret Jews and that because of it,

so much of value might be lost.
Please let me hear from you.

Shalom,
Trudi

▼▼▼

Simon's response came an hour later.

Tuesday, July 21, 1998
Dear Trudi,

Please, please, please don't worry! You never offended me with your
questions. In fact, your questions have made me think a lot about the facts
and myths of living a secret Jewish life.
I have so many things to tell you that I have to take a long time to
take it all off my head.
I am still thinking about the last question you asked me, because it is
pretty complex to explain the strange mix in secret Jewish rituals.
Please don't feel sad about asking. Only one who asks gets the answer.
I will write to you soon with a huge e-mail about Marranos' ways of
celebrating. . . .

Take care,
Simon

▼▼▼

The next letter came nearly a week later. He had been away again and just
returned from G-d only knows where.

Chapter Three

Monday, July 27, 1998
Trudi,

Well, I am back. Things have not been as good as they are supposed to be.
    One of the members of our community was discovered by his family and,
well, "the Inquisition is still working." We had to pull him out of the
country.

He added some disjointed facts about rituals, and ended with:

Well, I'll write you later. Take good care,
Simon

So, my dark intuition had been right. I wrote immediately.

Monday, July 27, 1998
Simon,

Even though you warned me, I cannot understand how this can still be happening!
I thought that the most serious threat facing secret Jews is the reaction from
mainstream Jews. But this case seems to be different.
    I assume from what you wrote that the family of the secret Jew must be Catholic,
so the potential danger must be coming from Catholics who don't want a Jew in the
family and don't want others to find out they are related to Jews. Am I right?
    What could they do to him that is serious enough to make him feel he had to
leave the country?
    You say "the Inquisition is still working." What does that mean?
    Does the Church have the power to really hurt a secret Jew? Or is it just his
Catholic relatives who would hurt him, privately, personally?
    What could they do to him? Why is there such fear? Are there any other secret
Jews in his family, and what will happen to them now?
    I know you may be too upset to answer all these questions now. Please, when you

are up to it, explain to me what happened and why.

Can I help?

Be well, Simon, and don't lose hope. Someday things will be different.

I pray for that every day.
Trudi

I had to wait another week before I heard from Simon again.

Monday, August 3, 1998
My dear friend Trudi,

I am back from _____. I traveled there to help my friend get settled, far away from any trouble.

I had to make the proper introductions to another secret Jewish community that I know. Everything is OK now.

I will write again tomorrow. There are many interesting things you should know.

Cheers,
Simon

Nearly another week passed, during which he was gone once more.

Sunday, August 9, 1998
Hi, there,

Well, I'm back again. Things took a little more time than I thought. But thank G-d, everything is OK now.

The situation was pretty serious. Try to imagine the reaction of these

Chapter Three

Catholic people finding out one of their family was a secret Jew!

The problem was not in the fact that they had a Jewish relative. It is based on the fact that he was A SECRET JEW!

If you are (openly) Jewish, you are respected as a member of a community. But being a secret Jew is another matter. You are considered an apostate, a disgrace to the Catholic Church.

Where is the tolerance in this XXth century? The reaction of this family made me think it was as bad as if they had found out their relative had AIDS!

In some ways the Inquisition is still here. You see, we still have to live in fear. When will the time of peace come?

OK. I will write you later.

Take care.
Shalom,
Simon

▼▼▼

It was not until six months later, with many letters in between, that Simon finally explained the reasons his friend had to flee the country after being unmasked.

I am placing part of that letter here, out of sequence.

Saturday, February 20, 1999

When I had to smuggle my friend out of the country because he was found out to be a Jew, people did not understand the concept of "secret Jew," but yes, they knew he was doing things in secret that were not precisely "Catholic issue."

Yes, he would have been shunned and thrown out of his family.

His godfather spoke about killing him because he did not want his godson living outside the "real and only true Church."

Would he be able to make a living? Of course not, not in this Catholic society.

CHAPTER THREE

When the trouble started, someone told him about me, and he came running to me, asking for help. He did not know [before] that one of the priests of his church was a secret Jew, and that one of his friends was also a secret Jew, but now he felt relief, he found peace. That's what I am here for, isn't it?

Try to imagine the rejection, the social pressure, people looking at him with skeptics' eyes.

Yes, his life was in danger. That does not mean that there is an official persecution against secret Jews, but when a case arises, you never know where intolerance will lead people.

In this part of the country, the struggle between Protestants and Catholics is very common, creating strong tensions. Not so much in the cities, but in the provinces, and sometimes people die because of this intolerance. But who they [the Christians] are is KNOWN. The fear of THE UNKNOWN is much more dangerous, and secret Jews fall into this category.

The danger does not come from the Church itself, but from inside Catholic families, inside Catholic society.

And if [a Crypto-Jew] cannot find support in a secret Jewish community, because he is not connected to one, and tries to get help from [mainstream] Jews, what is the answer, Trudi?

"Get out of here! You are not a Jew! You are a Catholic! You are a Goy, a Gentile!"

When was the last time Jews were rejected, insulted, threatened because they were Jews? Fifty years ago? Well, we suffer that fear every day of our lives. It is not racism. It is fear of the UNKNOWN, among Gentiles and Jews.

We will talk more on this issue.

Take some free time, Trudi, go take a coffee and think on the issue, walk around a park, think on the subject. . . .

Shabbat Shalom.
Simon

Chapter Four

During the next several weeks I heard very little from Simon.

In spite of my effort to keep a professional distance, I knew by the way I obsessively checked my e-mail that I was getting more emotionally involved with my subject than was usual or felt comfortable. Thus, because I was now more aware of how precarious Simon's position was, I worried about him.

When he finally did write, it was to let me know he would be out of town again, for a series of conferences in the United States.

On Friday, August 21, 1998, he sent a short note:

Trudi,

We have lived for centuries hidden and in fear . . . but every Friday night is a new chance to remember and understand the meaning of Shabbat, peace at last for us, the Anusim [a Hebrew term for secret Jews, meaning "the forced ones"], . . . and maybe, one of these days, Shabbat Shalom will be in Yerushalaim . . . at last!

I will write again before I leave.

Shalom,
Simon

▼▼▼

He didn't.

While Simon was gone, my grandson, Aaron (who was raised on a Buddhist ashram in Boulder, Colorado), called me all upset to tell me his car had been stolen.

"Do you still have that special connection with Saint Anthony, the one with

CHAPTER FOUR

the keys to the lost and found bureau in heaven? Could you ask him to find my car?"

Aaron remembered I had told him that while I lived at Marycliff, the nuns told me to pray to Saint Anthony if I was unable to find something I had misplaced. Whenever I did, the lost item somehow miraculously reappeared.

Turning to Saint Anthony to help me find lost things is one Catholic devotion I continued to hold on to long after I abandoned all others.

I told Aaron that anyone can approach this helpful saint, including a lapsed Catholic Jew, like me, or even a Buddhist. He agreed to give Saint Anthony a try.

Two weeks later Aaron called me again.

"Grandma, you forgot to warn me I had to tell Saint Anthony to find my car with the insides intact!"

The car had been found by the police, but it had been stripped down to the chassis!

I thought about this lingering attachment to something from my Catholic past while Simon was gone.

Turning to Saint Anthony for help did not in any way interfere with my self-identification as a Jew. Would that present a problem for Simon? I wondered.

When he returned, I sent off some related questions.

Tuesday, September 8, 1998
Simon,

Is there anything about the Catholic religion, dogmas, rituals that Crypto-Jews have been able to integrate into their beliefs and practices without compromising the integrity of their Jewishness?

Are you, yourself, able to bring any of your (Catholic) upbringing at home and at the seminary into your life as a Jew without spiritual conflict?

Please answer this as fully as you can.

Shalom,
Trudi

Chapter Four

Sunday, September 13, 1998
My dear Trudi,

You have asked one of the most difficult questions I have ever been asked.

This excellent question goes deep. I love to help you with your research, because I also learn a lot about my secret Jewish heritage. It's a two-way street. . . .

Even as a priest I sometimes have to deal with serious matters of behavior from people who come to me for advice.

As a secret Jew, you must always try to integrate your "normal" religious beliefs and practices without violating the integrity of your identity. But you must be careful: "integrating" does not mean that you accept them . . . ever!

You might find secret Jews who have accepted some Catholic traditions, and have learned to live with some kind of combination with them, but that is totally against the tradition of the Anusim.

Catholicism is just a way to hide ourselves, but we are JEWS! Our ancestors accepted Catholicism in order to protect the life, the tradition of the Jewish Sefarad (Spain) but we never really converted . . . that is different.

I, myself, as a priest, have had to deal every day of my life with a hard issue: doing things I don't believe in, may G-d forgive me.

Why would we call ourselves Anusim if we believe in the dogma of our hiddenness?

The life of a Crypto-Jew is not easy.

Many might try to make it easy, integrating into their Jewish beliefs new practices [thinking] it was not violating the integrity of their Jewishness. Don't you think our Jewishness is mixed up enough?

In a couple of weeks I will be going to the Vatican with a delegation of Latin American priests. There is a chance a XVIIIth-century priest will be canonized.

Take care,
Simon

Well, there it was, finally.

Simon had confirmed, ever so casually, that he was indeed a priest. (Although his first reference to this came in a letter I quoted earlier, it was written and dated much later than the one above.)

Now I felt I could at last tackle the issues that I have always found most difficult to understand.

Tuesday, September 15, 1998
Dear Simon,

What is the role, the function, the service that a Crypto-Jewish priest performs for his own people at such a tremendous personal sacrifice?

I know what his role was during the Inquisition, but I question if it could possibly be the same today.

Is the Crypto-Jewish priest's main purpose still to protect his people from hostile actions by the Church?

Does he try to influence other priests to be more tolerant, more accepting of Jews, speaking "from the inside, as one of their own," and do you believe he has any power to affect the attitude of the hierarchy by what he says and does?

Could he not spare himself the agony you describe by simply living as an ordinary, secret Jew? Or is the main intent of living as a priest to carry on an ancient tradition?

Good luck on your Vatican trip.
Trudi

Chapter Four

The response I got was short.

Tuesday, September 15, 1998
Trudi,

Let me think more on this question.
   What I can tell you so far is that, with or without a threat from the
Catholic Church, the role of the priesthood for a Crypto-Jew is to be as close
as he can to his own people, and to protect the values and heritage of our
fathers.

Take care.
Simon

▼▼▼

Simon's answer felt somehow flat, unconvincing. He seemed either unwilling
or unable to elaborate on or justify the meaning and value of what I saw as
a drastic, arbitrary, and soul twisting life sentence.

I knew this issue would have to be tackled again later.
I also realized I had lost my objectivity.

I was determined to try to be more careful, to remain as open, as impartial
as possible and refrain from injecting my own prejudices into my research.

When I heard nothing from Simon for several more days, I wrote to tell
him I would be on a research trip to Spain for two weeks, at about the same
time he would be at the Vatican.

On my return there still was no word from Simon.

Again it occurred to me he might just cut off, like Matthew. That experience had clearly left me feeling insecure about my connection with Simon.

Then he finally wrote again.

Chapter Four

Saturday, October 24, 1998
Dear Trudi,

I am back and it is good to be home again. I decided to take some time off to visit my mother in Spain.

And if I had known you were going to be in Spain, too, at that same time, we could have arranged a meeting! I made the mistake of not checking my e-mail before leaving.

I had a good time in Europe. I had the chance to visit some old friends and some places where I spent years studying at the seminary. It made me think a lot.

The research you are doing is a very complex issue, and you know I want to help you as much as I can, so let's start again.

Take care,
Simon

▼▼▼

Before Simon's next letter there came several days of silence while a hurricane swept through his area and disrupted his Internet service.

When he wrote again, he finally addressed some of my questions about the role the Crypto-Jewish priest assumes when ministering to the secret Jews in his parish.

Saturday, October 31, 1998
Trudi,

We are dealing with a very serious subject, the role of the secret priest in the secret Jewish community.

Since the time of the Inquisition, his role has become even more necessary, because he is the connection between the secret world of the Anusim and the outside world.

Chapter Four

*Not every priest has the same role. It depends on the community. The
community where I live is conformed of people who are almost 100 percent
Spanish or white Hispanic, not mixed race, very conservative, very Catholic,
and among them are secret Jewish families.*

*My role as a secret Jewish priest is to help these people live the hard life
they have, helping them understand and overcome the pain of living in fear
and anguish, and teaching them to be proud of their heritage.*

*Tell me if this is helping you with your arguments, ask me whatever
you feel. . . .*

Simon

▼▼▼

I now began to understand why there was such a difference between Simon's
perception of his priestly role and Matthew's: Simon lived within a secret
Jewish community whose members attended his church and his primary
responsibility was to them, rather than to his Catholic parishioners.

Matthew appeared to have no Jewish community, as such, to minister
to. He was isolated, hidden with his solitary secret Jewish identity in the
midst of his Catholic flock, who, of course, had no clue as to who he really was.

I was unable to ascertain if any secret Jews were among Matthew's flock
or what his personal duties to them might have been. If he had any interaction with secret Jews, they probably were individuals who sought him out
only if and when they needed him because they were in danger. Beyond
that, I am assuming that Matthew's responsibility to Crypto-Jews was to
keep tabs on the Church's activities.

Aside from members of the Orthodox Jewish community who, as it
turned out, never quite accepted Matthew and from whom he became
estranged after they rejected him, his day-to-day personal interaction was
restricted to his Catholic parishioners and his superiors in the diocese.

While Simon professed guilt over betraying his G-d when fulfilling his
priestly functions and was reluctant to reveal anything specific about his

interaction with the Catholic members of his parish, Matthew appeared at first to have no ethical conflict about holding himself out to be a priest.

He stressed that the only thing that mattered to him was knowing he was a Jew, living his private life according to ancient Jewish traditions and keeping Jewish laws. As far as he was concerned, being a priest was just a job. He managed to accept and live with this incongruity by somehow keeping his two functions and identities separate.

However, during one brief conversation, I discovered that Matthew's life as a priest was not as conflict-free as he had led me to believe. In order to make his day-to-day schizophrenic life more bearable, he had developed a strangely paternal relationship with his Catholic parishioners.

Once, when I asked him how he could reconcile his commitment to Judaism when his own life was spent as a Catholic priest performing Catholic rituals, Matthew's response sounded matter-of-fact:

"I minister to people who believe that the host and wine really become the body and blood of G-d. . . . I provide them with that. . . ."

The fact that he did not share their belief did not appear to bother him: they had theirs, he had his.

But then he added:

"Some of the new church laws are so ungodly.

"One of them forbids Catholics to kneel while receiving communion.

"Just think: a priest receiving the bishop's cap must kneel before the Pope, but a woman begging to kneel while receiving communion is refused. . . . She is humiliated before the congregation, is told to stand. . . .

"When she requests her bishop's permission to kneel, she is reprimanded, told she is wrong, and ordered to conform. . . .

"The Church callously ignores that these people believe in the old ways of respect and reverence for G-d. . . ."

I was surprised at the vehemence of Matthew's outrage at Mother Church's treatment of her own children. Clearly his allegiance was to them, not to the Catholic hierarchy. He seemed protective of those people and looked upon the Church authorities as their mutual adversary!

Chapter Four

I was still not convinced I had gotten down to the full psychological essence concerning this issue.

"How can you live with yourself," I probed, "knowing everything you do as a priest carries so much weight for those who are looking to you for Catholic spiritual guidance, while your own orientation and beliefs are those of a Jew?

"If they knew, would they not question whether the sacraments you performed were valid? Would they not wonder if your absolutions wiped out their sins? Would they not worry whether their children were legitimate if you had married them? Do you not feel you are betraying their trust?"

Again his answer was simple and surprising.

"What I believe does not matter. I am an ordained priest. The sacraments I perform are valid. Once a priest, always a priest. What I do is a mitzvah. I help them worship what they believe is G-d. . . .

"Just think . . . they get close to G-d with the help of a Jewish rabbi! Who cares how, as long they reach out to G-d and honor Him. . . . I make it possible for them to do that. . . ."

Then he paused, and a strange expression came into his eyes.

"But when I have to bless medals en masse, do confession duty, do baptisms, then the conflict becomes overwhelming. . . . I go home and, for two days afterward, I cannot stand . . . or eat. . . . I throw up and go to bed. . . ."

Author's note: I contacted Father Andrew Greeley, a well-known and respected Catholic priest, sociologist, and author, to ask him: "How true is the statement 'Once a priest, always a priest'? How about a defrocked or excommunicated one? What about a Crypto-Jewish priest who was legally ordained but remained a secret Jew? Are the sacraments administered by any of the above valid? Does a priest's own orientation, belief system, or doubts affect the validity of his ministrations?"

Father Greeley's response was: "The Church believes that the validity of a sacrament is not dependent on the virtue of the minister."

CHAPTER FIVE

As I asked more and more questions, I had to accept the fact that Simon was so uncomfortable with his activities serving his Catholic parishioners as their priest that he was unable or unwilling to respond to that issue with any meaningful detail.

He had emphasized again and again that aside from his day-to-day mandatory duties as a member of the Catholic clergy, his primary responsibility was to the large number of secret Jews within his parish: to serve them, be their spiritual guide, and be the intermediary between them and the Church. Living a lie was the only way he could keep that commitment.

The more Simon told me, the less the way he lived his life made sense to me. Despite my effort to remain neutral, I could not suppress my consternation. How could an ethical social or religious system encourage someone to live such a conflicted life, demanding that he split his soul by keeping his very essence secret? I struggled with my conscience, wondering if it was fair of me to burden Simon with my growing skepticism, but I finally decided that I had no choice if we were to maintain the authenticity and honesty of our mutual exploration.

Wednesday, November 4, 1998
Simon,

If, as you say, the role of the priest is to alleviate his people's anguish, to help them "be proud of their heritage," etc., why does he have to be a priest to do that?

Please forgive me for being so persistent about this issue, but during my lectures, when I talk about the Crypto-Jewish tradition of mandating one male member of each generation to join the Church, the most frequent question I am asked is one for which I have no answer:

Chapter Five

"Why does he have to be a priest?"

Does his presence as a member of the clergy accomplish anything more than what he could do as well, or even better, as a rabbi or just a spiritual leader of his secret Jewish community?

The issue I find most difficult to explain is that as a Catholic priest, a secret Jew is forced to pretend to support the beliefs, laws, and precepts of the Catholic Church if he wants to avoid being found out. This must be a terrible conflict of conscience, an unbearably difficult emotional as well as spiritual ordeal to live with daily!

UNLESS A SECRET JEW BRINGS A COMPELLING UNIQUE BENEFIT TO HIS COMMUNITY BY LIVING OUTWARDLY AS A PRIEST, IS THAT NOT A NEEDLESS SACRIFICE???

Please answer this.
Trudi

▼▼▼

Weeks passed during which the hurricane wreaked havoc in Simon's area. In one of his brief letters during that time he described how he had to spend day after day ministering to the wounded and helping to bury hundreds of dead.

When I asked if he was safe, all he was willing to volunteer was:

"Don't worry. I am not in Honduras!"

Thanksgiving came and went. Simon either ignored my challenge concerning the functional need for present-day Crypto-Jewish priests or forgot all about the questions during the tumult created by the hurricane.

Convinced that this was too uncomfortable a topic for him to face, I went on to other relatively underexplored issues.

I kept writing, asking questions, looking for more detailed facts about his childhood, his family, knowing that sometimes I had to repeat myself again and again . . . hoping . . . trusting that eventually, Simon would come through . . . if he was all right.

CHAPTER FIVE

Finally, after a month's silence, he made contact again and responded to some of my earlier questions.

Tuesday, December 1, 1998
Hi there again, Trudi,

I was invited for Thanksgiving at some American friends' house, a very special evening.

I think the essence of this celebration should be understood by more people. It is good to get together with friends and family, and give thanks for good things received during the year.

More about my family: my mother and all her family are Spaniards, Catholics, and they have no idea about my identity.

My father is Catholic too, and he does not know about my secret life either, because in my family (my father's side) the only ones who have lived this life are my grandfather and my uncle (the first son in his generation), but my uncle never got married, so after he died the tradition was passed on to me.

As I told you, my family arrived in _____ around the XVIIth century as normal Spanish immigrants, but they had already converted. They changed their name and settled in a Marrano community, but, of course, other people thought this was a normal Spanish ghetto in New Spain.

By the XIXth century it was very difficult to maintain a secret Jewish identity in _____ , at least where my family settled.

You must remember that _____ has always been a very Catholic country. Some of my ancestors were judged by the Inquisition when it was established here and died as "conversos" or "Judios." But they never lost their Sephardic heritage, they spoke Ladino and celebrated Judaism according to the Sephardic way.

So, my grandfather, as one of the elders of the Marrano community, established the rule that only the firstborn (male) child would carry the responsibility of keeping our tradition.

Chapter Five

By the way, my grandfather married a Spanish Catholic woman, which caused him a lot of trouble, and that is why he moved here.

My father (who knew nothing about his own father's secret Jewishness) also married a Spanish Catholic girl (my mother), very, very Catholic. I was raised as a regular Catholic kid until, at the age of twelve, I was introduced by my grandfather to this secret life of ours.

He told me all about the history of our people and the big responsibility I was receiving. Like any Jewish kid, I had a Bar Mitzvah. But it was secret. That day, when I put on the tallith and the tefillin, I cried during the ceremony, praying the oldest and most holy prayer of our people, Shema Israel. . . .

I was in the theological seminary for almost eight years. Now I serve as assistant priest in our community of 300, in _____, but I only personally know about 150 of the secret Jews. My biggest task is to help them live this life.

I am sorry for this long e-mail.

Take care,
Simon

▼▼▼

Months later, Simon finally described in greater detail how he found out about his true identity and how he dealt with his transformation from "a Catholic kid" to the secret Jew he has become.

I insert parts of two of those letters here, again out of sequence:

Friday, April 9, 1999

After my Bar Mitzvah (which was held in the traditional, but secret way), my grandfather told my (Catholic) father it would be a great idea to send me to a religious school in Spain, and offered that of course he would take care of me.

That is how I happened to go to the Continent, and entered into a different world: the world of the Catholic Church.

CHAPTER FIVE

I was required to stay in the boarding school from Monday to Friday noon. Then I had the chance to visit my grandfather, and it was on those weekends I learned all about the secret life of the hidden Jews. It was then he taught me every detail of the Jewish faith.

Every morning at school I was required to pray, to recite the "Pater Nostri," "Salve Maria," and "Salve Regina." Then there were about eight hours of classes and homework. The schedule included Church history, Latin, classical philosophy, logic, world history, English, French.

At the age of almost sixteen I skipped the last year of school and entered the seminary.

This not only required a great effort and academic skills, but every person had to prove a spiritual life, a spiritual commitment to the Catholic Church. I struggled a lot with this.

No ritual, no act, no song meant anything to me. All I wanted was to return every Friday afternoon to my grandfather's house, to celebrate the Shabbat.

So try to imagine, Trudi, how my heart rejoiced when my grandfather started to light the candles, when he began to sing the songs welcoming the Shabbat, with our faces turned to Jerusalem, the sun going down, saying the Shema.

Enough for now, too many memories are coming alive.

Simon

He continued to elaborate on this matter in part of this second letter, dated March 14, 1999.

Concerning your questions about my childhood, I don't know how helpful my answers will be.

I was not really a normal kid. . . . I was rebellious, always getting into trouble, not very aware of what it meant to be Catholic. I never paid much attention during mass or in catechism classes.

Chapter Five

Sunday mornings were always hard times for me because I knew I would not be able to see the soccer games, especially if the Real Madrid were playing.

Religion was not a very important part in my life. I always used to say bullfights were my religion. . . . Today, when I sometimes attend bullfights as a normal person, when I sit, light my cigar, I do miss what I gave away so long ago, MY FREEDOM OF BEING MYSELF, OF BEING NORMAL.

Maybe that is why my grandfather chose me, because being Catholic was never a strong part of me. I didn't give a damn about the issues of Christians and Jews at that time, so, when I was told I was a Jew, it didn't matter to me. Actually, when I realized that being a Jew meant I was not Catholic, I became a happy kid!

However, I cannot explain the change that came over me later, when I came in contact with the ceremoniosity [sic] of the secret Jewish services, with the lyrics, and the music, and the rites, with the beauty and the mysticism that was there. . . . I just can say it got to me. . . .

And then, seeing my grandfather bowing up and down, covered in his long, white prayer shawl, with the tefillin on him, whispering words I could not understand, I understood what, who I was.

And when the time came and I had to choose between a normal life and the life I now have, I was able to give it all away, for what my people are.

Shalom,
Simon

▼▼▼

Even before I received those two letters, the way Simon described how he felt about embracing his Jewishness and his willingness to abandon a normal life had a profound effect on me. It brought back old, old feelings: the nostalgia of remembering myself, at nineteen, so filled with a need for a connection with G-d and religious zeal that I was willing, eager, to give up all worldly pleasures to become a missionary nun.

By December 1998 Simon and I had been corresponding for six months.

CHAPTER FIVE

I felt deeply connected to his spirit and thought of him as the quintessential "old soul."

I kept wishing I could talk to him face-to-face and tried to conjure up a psychic vision of him: I imagined this tall, slim, white-haired man, probably in his sixties, with fine chiseled features reminiscent of El Greco portraits of martyred saints I had seen in Toledo, his deep-set dark eyes full of pain.

I, a seventy-one-year-old grandmother, had to laugh at my girlish effort to romanticize him and quickly dismissed my fantasy. "He's probably much older, pudgy, and not at all ascetic looking."

In mid-December Simon wrote to tell me he was going to Canada.

> *I always need to see some snow this time of year. Even a secret Jew needs a vacation sometime!*
> *Don't worry, you'll hear from me again.*

On his return after New Year's he was eager to resume our correspondence:

> *For sure, we must start again our discussions.*
> *Simon*

Now I was ready to once more remind Simon that he had not yet answered my questions about the need for the existence of present-day Crypto-Jewish priests. Did he forget, or was he still avoiding the issue?

I thought that perhaps now that he had a rest, he'd be more willing to tackle the subject. I was determined to keep repeating my probes until I had an answer that had some conviction behind it. I ended my long litany of questions with a casual aside:

> *By the way, while you are on vacation, are you able to shed your priestly role and just be your real self? I hope so!*
> *Trudi*

Chapter Five

His response was immediate.

> *Sunday, January 10, 1999*
> *Trudi,*
>
> *One short answer to one of your questions, before I take on the rest: "Am I able to shed my priestly role on vacation and just be my real self?" YOU BET! I need to have a normal life. Those are my only chances to (openly) attend a synagogue and interact and live a normal Jewish life!*
>
> *Simon*

The vacation clearly had been good for him. How different he sounded!

> *Thursday, January 14, 1999*
> *Dear Simon,*
>
> *Your last letter made me laugh! You sounded like a kid who had broken out of jail! How long have you been a priest?*
> *Shalom,*
> *Trudi*

Next day I wrote again. I was concerned that I had become a little too casual and was afraid I might have offended him with my familiarity.

> *Friday, January 15, 1999*
> *Dear Simon,*
>
> *Please excuse my last letter. It was pretty disrespectful.*
> *After reading your "you bet" letter, I realized how little I actually know about*

you! You suddenly sounded so young, so joyful, so full of life, so different from the often tormented man I have come to know through your previous letters, that it took me by surprise.

I was so happy to see that change, so glad you sometimes have the opportunity to live a normal life. So, if my relief came across in an inappropriate way, forgive me.

Trudi

Simon's response came less than an hour later.

Friday, January 15, 1999
Trudi,

Don't worry, you were not disrespectful. I felt happy when you treated me a little more in confidence, more personally.

Yes, it is true. I am a tormented man, and my only happy times come when I can live a normal life.

Simon

I felt relieved but once again noticed I had received no response to my many questions about the relevance of the Crypto-Jewish priesthood.

Tuesday, January 19, 1999
Dear Simon,

Unless you are very busy, my last questions must be giving you a lot of trouble, since you have not answered them. So, here come some easier ones, for now:

Can you tell me what it was like to be at the seminary?
How long were you there?
Were you close to your family in Spain?

Did you have any close calls while there, when your real identity came into question?

What was the most difficult part for you?

What did you do to preserve your Jewish soul under such close scrutiny?

I hope the freedom you enjoyed during your vacation sustains you for a long time!

Shalom!
Trudi

P.S. Well, these questions should be easier to answer since they do not require you to examine your present life!

▼▼▼

Thursday, January 21, 1999
Trudi,

I have been having difficulty answering your questions, not because they are difficult but because of an electrical problem that damaged my computer.

Being at the seminary is one of the things I feel most guilty about.

It is not only the matter of attending mass every day, it is the idea of adopting as my own values and traditions [those] that for centuries were the reason why so many of my own people were murdered.

And yes, there were times I wanted to quit, to forget the pressures and the responsibilities I had to carry. I went to the seminary in order to become, in the future, the spiritual leader of my community.

You have to understand that I was a boy when I was trained in the customs and traditions of the Marrano life. When I learned what was needed of me, I went into the seminary.

Despite the fact that my mother's family lived not far, I never called them. I never let them know I was there because I needed to defeat my inner contradictions alone, so that later, in the future, I would be able to help others who chose to live the same life.

What was the most difficult part of it for me? What did I do to preserve my Jewish soul under such close scrutiny???

And you call these questions EASY? My G-d!!

The hardest thing was not only pretending I believed that my salvation was placed on a church that has blood on her hands, bowing myself before images, reciting empty words every day, the same words that led many of my people to their death, carrying with me the cross as a symbol of salvation. It was the fact that I had to put into the dark the things I love, the things that made me what I am now, AN ANUSIM!

I did this for almost eight years. I am now twenty-five years old.

I stopped reading, in shock. TWENTY-FIVE YEARS OLD!!! A boy!

If he entered the seminary at fifteen and spent nearly eight years there before ordination, he had been a priest for only two years! I read on:

How did I survive in the seminary?

I would say I tied myself as hard as I could, to the idea of one G-d, Shema Israel, Adonai Eloheynu Ehad, Ehad!!!!!

There is a time in life when these words become more than a prayer. It is true that secret Jews do not survive, they adapt, keeping in the dark what they really are.

Simon

▼▼▼

I burst into tears.

CHAPTER SIX

It took a long time to absorb and relate to Simon's last letter. When it finally registered, I remained overwhelmed with sadness.

What a waste!

This was not the mature man I had seen in my mind's eye. He was a young boy, forced to lead this abnormal life, burdened down not only with tremendous responsibilities, but in constant fear of the consequences if he failed to keep his own identity as well as those of his flock safely hidden. All that while struggling to help them, as well as himself, to stay afloat spiritually, as Jews.

Anger surged up in me at the very thought that any tradition could justify expecting anyone to make such a personal sacrifice so early in life and for so long.

It also occurred to me that I now had to adjust my inner image of Simon. That made me smile, a little ruefully. So much for fantasies!

Now I was determined to get answers! Answers that made sense!

Friday, January 22, 1999
Dear Simon,

I can't believe you are only twenty-five years old! You're too young to have carried such a huge burden for half of your life, spending eight years twisted into a pretzel, living among those you have always considered your people's enemies, pretending to be one of them.

What is the purpose of a Crypto-Jewish priest giving up a normal life to live in a way that goes against everything he believes and values, without even the support of his own family?

WHO BENEFITS FROM THIS? HAS HE NOT NOW BECOME

CHAPTER SIX

AN ANACHRONISM??? Please answer this!
Trudi

▼▼▼

Simon's next letter did not even address me by name.

Saturday, January 23, 1999

NO! I don't believe the life of the Crypto-Jewish priest has become an anachronism at all.

Perhaps other secret Jews have accepted the Christian faith during their time in the priesthood, but that is not true for me. That would not help me, or any other secret Jews.

We have to accept the fact that the life of the secret Jew is hard, complex, and sad. Someone has to be there for them, someone who not only understands their pain, but has himself experienced and overcome the circumstances that every secret Jew experiences.

Maybe some of them will never come to me, talk to me, and maybe you will think that those eight years of my life were wasted. But I am here to help them overcome their struggles, open to their needs whenever they need to come.

That's my life.

Simon

▼▼▼

I was taken aback by the passion in Simon's response. When I responded, it was with a sad, new respect for his young soul.

Saturday, January 23, 1999
Simon,

I am finally beginning to understand, and accept, that being a Crypto-Jewish priest is not a matter of logic or reason. It is a matter of the heart, of commitment to a tradition that transcends intellectual explanations. . . .

My brain will take a while to sort all this out, but my heart has heard you at last. . . .

So, no more questions tonight . . . more later.

Shalom,
Trudi

▼▼▼

I finally realized that I had to stop prodding, stop asking Simon to justify himself to himself and to me.

This was, after all, HIS life.

But I could not get his letter out of my mind all weekend long.

Then I began to understand.

Not Simon.

Myself.

I wrote an amendment to my last letter.

Monday, January 25, 1999
Dear Simon,

For the first time since we began our dialogue, I felt I made you upset, even perhaps angry, with one of my questions.

The last few days I had to ask myself: Why have I been so persistent, insisting that you prove to yourself, and to me, that your life as a priest has meaning, that there is valid relevance in your having to lie about who you really are day after day?

Was it really only the historical investigator in me looking for a credible, logical answer I could support and offer when challenged? Or was there something else, something more personal pushing me to pressure you?

Well, after all these years, I finally realize I am still struggling with unfinished private business: the still lingering guilt and shame I felt for so long for denying I was a Jew in order to survive the Holocaust, while other millions died.

For me, finding out I was a Jew (at about the same age you did), and then denying it and hiding under a Catholic cover, felt like the ultimate sin of betrayal.

It took years of therapy to come to terms with my "apostasy" and feel entitled to call myself a Jew. I thought I had succeeded . . . until now.

My psychic connection with Crypto-Jews like yourself is based on the fact that you do what I did: lie, pretend, hide the truth in order to survive. . . .

But unlike me, you have somehow been able to keep your connection with G-d, with centuries of tradition to sustain you, while I still can't quite forgive myself. A small part of me still feels I should have died.

My dialogue with you has opened that old wound.

Please forgive me for expecting you to heal that for me. The therapist in me should have recognized what was happening. . . .

Now that I know, I should be able to handle this better. I hope I have not hurt you with all this pressure.

Shalom,
Trudi

▼▼▼

Again, Simon's answer came an hour later.

Monday, January 25, 1999
Trudi,

Don't be worried. I never get angry as a result of your questions. I love talking to you. That is why you always get an answer from me. Sometimes it might seem that I am angry, but that is just my Spanish way.

Don't worry. I also have been able to heal some of my wounds because of our talks: I know there is someone out there that understands me.

Best and love,
Simon

Chapter Six

I finally felt we were at peace with our mutual work and with each other.

Again, days went by without a word from Simon. One week, two weeks. I began to worry again. Did someone find out about him? Did he have to run away and hide, like his friend?

Finally, another letter.

Friday, February 12, 1999
Trudi,

You must be wondering where the hell am I, right? Well, last weekend I went to a bullfight in _____ (I am a religious fan of bullfights).

Then last Tuesday I got appendicitis, and I've been in the hospital since then! I am OK now.

Don't worry, if I have to disappear one of these days, I will let you know.

Simon

A subtle and welcome reminder that I was dealing with a very young man. . . .

At about this time a small but prestigious publishing house expressed interest in bringing out a book that featured my correspondence with Simon, but the editors were concerned about Simon's insistence on remaining anonymous.

I told Simon about it and asked if he would be willing to give me a release, with his real full name, allowing me to use excerpts from his letters.

I reminded him that I had kept my word to Matthew and never revealed his identity or whereabouts. I was hopeful that I would eventually convince the publishers that Simon's need for secrecy was justified.

CHAPTER SIX

Wednesday, February 17, 1999
Well, Trudi, I am glad to hear your news.

It is a great opportunity for you, a great prize for your efforts and your excellent job as a researcher.

But to be honest with you, I am very skeptical about the idea of making public our conversations. Only if you promise not to reveal my name, my locality, and any other data that might give an idea of who I am, you will have my permission to do what you want to do.

You have to understand what would happen if people around me find out who I am, and what I am. I would have to run away, and I don't want to have to run away. Especially because it would hurt my mother and my family, who are typical Spaniards and very Catholic.

If you can assure me of these requirements, to keep my identity secret, you have my word and my permission.

Because, as a friend, I trust you.

"I, _____ _____ _____ , give Trudi Alexy permission to use excerpts from my letters for publication, without revealing my identity, for the good of my people.

Dated: February 17, 1999"

I never knew his full name before and could only imagine what he must have felt knowing the risk involved in revealing himself to me.

Wednesday, February 17, 1999
Dear Simon,

Thank you for trusting me.

I shall continue to delete our correspondence and keep your letters in a locked metal case. Every identifying name or location is blacked out.

Chapter Six

Now that I have a specific assignment, we will have to go over some of the questions that remain unanswered. May G-d help me to do a good job.

I want to show what your world is like and why you and your people deserve compassion and understanding, instead of persecution and rejection.

Thank you again,
Trudi

▼▼▼

Simon's response surprised me. It should not have, since I've lived in Spain and know the Spanish male psyche rather well.

Thursday, February 18, 1999
Trudi,

I am putting my life in your hands. Please ask me again what you need to know.

Just one point: the secret Jewish people are not asking for compassion and understanding instead of persecution and rejection.

I don't want anyone to think we are looking for affirmative action. We just need respect for what we are: recognition for our heritage, because we are Jews.

We don't need conversion and extra rituals to prove that we are Jews. We keep the law . . . in secret.

Shalom,
Simon

▼▼▼

Here is a perfect example of that indomitable Spanish pride . . . head high, knowing the value of his beliefs, his identity, unwilling to tolerate pity or anything less than what he believes is his just due.

Even his people's expulsion from Spain and dispersion throughout a hostile world could not kill that.

Now that I had the green light from Simon, I immediately went ahead with more fundamental questions.

Thursday, February 18, 1999
Dear Simon,

A prominent Sephardic rabbi who has a lot of experience dealing with Crypto-Jewish issues took me to task after my first book was published for advocating tolerance and acceptance of Crypto-Jews as legitimate Jews by the mainstream Jewish community.

I am paraphrasing his words:

"Because centuries of secrecy make it difficult to prove that an individual secret Jew has kept all the requisite halakhist laws or that matrilineal Jewishness was maintained and kept unbroken all the way back, a Crypto-Jew must go through the official conversion process, just to make sure.

"Even if his family's oral history indicates his claims are true, if he is really serious about declaring himself a Jew and living a Jewish life, he should not object to doing this."

The example he gave me to prove his point is:

"Imagine that someone writes to our Immigration Department and says: `Although I am a citizen of a foreign country, I have always been an American, secretly, in my heart, and so has my family. I want to be accepted as an American citizen.'

"The Immigration Department would say to him: 'If you want to be an American citizen, you have to follow a certain protocol.

"'You have to come here, take classes and learn our laws, pass a test, and be naturalized, and then we will give you all the benefits of citizenship. You will get an American passport and you will be allowed to vote.

"'No matter what you claim in your heart, not until then will we consider you an American citizen entitled to all the rights, privileges, and protection under our laws.'"

Another prominent but more liberal rabbi, in response to my question about the relevance and intent of the Kol Nidre, as it might apply to Crypto-Jews, told me: "That prayer is meant to forgive Jews for vows denying their Jewishness, BUT

ONLY IF THERE IS REAL DANGER."

When I countered that Crypto-Jews have always felt they are in danger, he protested that this is an unreasonable position.

"Claiming they are in danger now is not enough of an excuse for denying that they are Jews. During the Inquisition and the Holocaust, yes, it was valid, but not today."

Of course these were both Orthodox rabbis, and I suspect there are more liberal ones, from perhaps Reform or even Conservative congregations, who might be willing to make some concessions. So far as I know, only one has been willing to offer an alternative to conversion, a "Ceremony of Return."

Simon, you must know what my position is: like you, I have a lot of doubts, a lot of questions.

Although many Jews in Israel are secular, never attend services, and do not practice any of the Jewish laws or traditions, how come they have no problems proving their identities as Jews?

How is it that these nonaffiliated Jews are nevertheless accorded all the privileges a Jew is entitled to, including the "right of return" to their Jewish homeland, and are fully accepted as Jews according to both religious and secular laws?

Where is the fairness in singling out for exclusion secret Jews who express a desire to emerge into the light after centuries in the dark? These Jews claim a history of family observance and martyrdom. Why are they required to convert to be accepted as Jews?

I guess my real question is: WHERE IS G-D IN ALL THIS?

Why is the fact that one's mother is a Jew enough to automatically make even an atheist a Jew?

Why is the fact that you are living a deeply religious Jewish life in your heart and soul, keeping age-old family traditions, considered irrelevant just because you were born of a Gentile mother?

HOW CAN THIS BE OUR LAW???

Please respond to the rabbis I quoted above.

Shalom,
Trudi

CHAPTER SIX

Simon's response seethed with sarcasm.

Thursday, February 18, 1999
Trudi,

OK!

    So, if a Crypto-Jew cannot prove all the mothers in his family were Jews, he has to go through the conversion process?

    How good it is to know this! Since we are not Jews, we have been persecuted for nothing!

    How stupid we were, pretending we are Jews all this time! We were never really Jews, so we obviously died in vain!

    The next time someone comes to me arguing about the rights of secret Jews, I will tell him, "Hey, don't talk to me about this, I'm not really a Jew! I am a freak who worships as a Catholic and prays as a Jew!"

    I do not agree with the principles of modern rabbinism. Even an atheist is considered a Jew as long as he has a Jewish mother, born of her blood.

    Do we have racism among Jews, accepting there is a Jewish race?

    Are we Jewish because of a ritual, because it is done only a certain way??? Or because we believe and keep the essence of the ritual???

    I am a Jew. My ancestors burned in the fire because they were Jews, with or without the recognition of modern Judaism!

    What about people who died in concentration camps, who never attended a synagogue, never had any relationship to their religion? Why are they Jews more than I?

    Because their names were Stein or Rosenberg?

    This sounds familiar, does it not? German Jews lost their rights and citizenship as a result of the Nazi Nuremberg laws.

    The identity of being Jewish goes beyond rituals.

    We are tied to the essence of the faith, because it is part of what we are . . . a biblical Judaism. We seek a mystical experience with G-d, we do not put

Chapter Six

our attention on the way a ritual is conducted.

The concept of being a secret Jew goes further than merely having a certain feeling in our heart. . . .

We are raised in a certain way, educated according to specific principles for a purpose, for one reason: to protect what we are.

Trudi, this is an argument we have had for five hundred years: Catholics accusing us of being Jews, and Jews arguing that we are not!

Tell the rabbi who explained the official position on the Kol Nidre to come down here and live where I live!

If he says there is not enough danger, that there is not enough of a reason to hide we are Jews, I will tell him that I guess there is no need for the efforts of the Wiesenthal Foundation, because there no longer is any danger from racism or anti-Semitism in our days.

Ah, sorry . . . I forgot, the danger does exist, but only for REAL JEWS! Who gets to define who is a Jew? Gentiles? Jews? Or G-d??

Give me more time to think on these issues.

Simon

▼▼▼

I felt helpless. What could I say to soothe his pain and righteous anger?

Friday, February 19, 1999
Dear Simon,

Please do not confuse me with the skeptics: I am on your side! I believe you, but I am trying to find a way to show to others that your people's traditions are valid and real, so that you will get the acceptance and respect you deserve.

Please write more about all this, if you can stand it, and please don't run away the way Matthew did. Let us fight this battle together.

Please tell me what happened to the man you had to smuggle out of the country when his family discovered he was a secret Jew. What would have happened if he had stayed? Would he be treated like the German Jews under the Nuremberg laws? Would he be killed? Would he be shunned the way the Mormons do it?

Please write,
Trudi

It is at this point that Simon wrote the letter from which I quoted a segment earlier, in which he described in detail what would have happened to that man if he had not been spirited out of the country: his godfather talked of killing him, he would have been shunned, prevented from making a living and rejected by his family, by both Jews and Catholics.

Here is the rest of that letter.

Saturday, February 20, 1999
Trudi, Trudi, my dear Trudi,

I know you are on my side! Don't worry. That is the reason I decided to get in touch with you.

If one of these days I decide to "come out" and if I need to convert, I will go with you.

Simon

▼

Then came a calmer follow-up.

Monday, February 22, 1999
Trudi,

We should have a coffee, and discuss these issues, as we do in Europe. We fix the world's problems in cafés.

It is a fact that all religions have their laws and requirements for

Chapter Six

inclusion, some basic criteria to define who is who.

Take the Church, for example, which is first of all a political society.

You find the positions in their hierarchy based on power.

They help to maintain the Church's power.

People are tied to that institution by means of a membership, based in this case on a basic belief, like the Apostles' Creed.

You believe and belong or you are an outsider.

For Jews, the argument about acceptance of certain traditions, common practices that unite our people, the basic idea of being "chosen," of receiving commandments and promises, is all valid.

So I ask: DON'T WE, THE SECRET JEWS, ALSO HAVE OUR TRADITIONS? COMMON PRACTICES?

DON'T WE BELIEVE IN THE CONCEPT OF ONE G-D, CREATOR OF HEAVEN AND EARTH?

DON'T WE OBSERVE THE PRINCIPLES AND STATUTES OF THE LAW, OF A NORM OF LAW REQUIRED BY G-D?

You can find the thirteen principles of faith explained by Maimonides in the common practices of the secret Jews.

So, it is NOT true that all we have is "a deep feeling of being Jews."

The problem is that OUR JUDAISM IS NOT ENOUGH BECAUSE MAINSTREAM JEWS DO NOT ACCEPT IT!

You asked once: Is the fact that a secret Jew's ancestors died for their faith enough to make him a Jew, and is just his desire to be a Jew enough?

For us, the secret Jews, the simple answer is YES!

To what else can we tie ourselves? What else is left?

After centuries and centuries of keeping our identities secret, centuries after centuries of teaching our sons and grandsons to live this life, to observe G-d's laws, what is their [mainstream Jews'] judgment?" NOT VALID!

Not valid because you didn't do it the mainstream way, because it was done in secret, because you did it after mass, etc. . . . What else is left, Trudi?

What would happen if tomorrow the Orthodox rabbinate decides that all Reform Jews are not Jews? Would that be valid?

Chapter Six

What are we? Maybe to outsiders we are Marranos, BUT INSIDE WE ARE JEWS.

Simon

Two days later, as if to lend more weight to his argument, Simon followed up that letter with another one revealing startling new information, opening up a painful part of his life he clearly wished he could forget.

Monday, February 22, 1999

Two short answers on issues I don't want to bring up again.
*   1. My grandfather used to lead services until he died. With his death the normal attendance of his secret services declined. He died before I came back from the seminary. My goal is to gain the confidence of the old community, to revive them, to start again.*
*   2. My uncle (who was the family priest before me) was murdered by Jews. That's all I have to say.*

Simon

Shocked as I was, I realized that knowing about this hate crime immediately placed me in a precarious professional double bind.

I did not want to pressure Simon to return to something as painful as his uncle's murder, but I could not allow this allegation to remain so vague, so unexplained.

Chapter Six

Friday, February 26, 1999
Dear Simon,

What a horror! I can only imagine the effect it must have on you, even now.

I am trying to stick to my commitment to respect your decision to withhold anything you did not want to discuss, but, while I have the utmost sympathy for how difficult it must be for you to talk about this, I also feel you must have had a reason for telling me about your uncle's murder.

I long ago committed myself to telling the truth, to present your people's authentic voice. You have given me that opportunity as no one else.

That is why I hope that someday you will want to tell me more about what happened, give some pertinent details, and not just let that bomb lie where you dropped it.

Simon, I send you peace.

Shalom,
Trudi

▼▼▼

I did not really expect to hear more about any of this for a long time, if ever. . . .

But I should by now have known that Simon is often unpredictable, always surprising. His response came that same afternoon.

Friday, February 26, 1999
Trudi,

I love every Friday afternoon. It is the only time when I can finally feel peace.

I love it when, in the closeness of my home, in secret, I light my candles, say the prayer, and receive the Shabbat. That is what the Shabbat means: Shabbat Shalom, peace at last, peace this day . . . the day when I can be what I am, a Jew.

Chapter Six

Please don't worry about my struggles and the tragedies of my life. I don't want anyone to feel my bitterness and my sadness in their hearts. They are buried.

The fact that two young radical Ashkenazi men murdered my uncle because they felt his being a priest was a dishonor and a joke to Judaism is something I don't want to remember.

It is in the past. But the intolerance toward secret Jews comes from both Gentiles and Jews. The case of my uncle is just the extreme of an attitude we must stop.
On both sides.
Rest, Trudi.

Shabbat Shalom.
Simon

CHAPTER SEVEN

Nearly two weeks passed without any further word from Simon.

It was hard not to worry. I had to keep reassuring myself that he was OK, that he had learned well the art of hiding, of wearing his mask, of keeping himself safe.

How different it had been for me, when I first wore my own mask. As a child of eleven, I had worn it fearlessly, with no concerns. Because my parents protected me, shielded me from anything that might reveal the precariousness of our situation as Jewish refugees masquerading as Catholics in a Fascist country, I did not discover until years later what life had really been like for them.

Although history later revealed that Spain proved to be a safe haven for masses of unbaptized Jews during the Holocaust, my parents never felt secure. They did not know from one day to the next when Franco would obey Hitler's repeated demands that he send back the Jews who had begun to pour into Spain by the thousands or would agree to at least put into effect the racial laws to which all Fascist-dominated countries were expected to submit.

Would the Spanish authorities become suspicious, accept our baptismal certificates or question their authenticity?

Would they send us back?

These questions were always on my parents' minds. The presence of German soldiers and German propaganda films bragging about Nazi victories served to reinforce their fear.

I was not aware of any of this and loved my carefree years in Barcelona. What did it matter that I had to spend long hours in food lines every day, waiting to buy two potatoes, some sugar, or a small pitcher of olive oil? I did not mind because it was almost like a game, with everyone in the same boat.

Chapter Seven

Our landlady's maid, Pilar, was a magician in the kitchen. Although some foods, like meat and bread, were scarce, a fisherman friend occasionally provided her with part of his daily catch, and she always managed to have a delicious meal on the table for Senora Carron and my family.

Most importantly, I felt I had resolved my guilt over abandoning my recently discovered Jewish identity by adopting a new one that filled me with hope and wonder and promised me forgiveness and redemption. My Catholic mask allowed me to feel safe.

It was clear that Simon never felt safe under his.

Toward mid-March Simon announced he had not had time to write because he was busy preparing material for a series of lectures to theology students at a university in a neighboring country.

"I have to be especially well prepared," he explained, "since I look so young for a 'visiting speaker.'"

I wrote to tell him two publishers had turned down my book proposal, because they felt I did not have enough concrete, verifiable facts to prove Simon was real and his story true. Several recent book scandals had made them overly cautious. I wished there were a way to meet him in person. . . . I decided to broach that subject slowly.

Sunday, March 14, 1999
Dear Simon,

Good luck on your seminars.

I so wish we could meet face-to-face. It would make my task so much easier if we could just talk. . . .

I want to know how you live, what are your duties as a priest, do you have friends, a social life?

Do you always have to go away to live normally, or is there a safe place for you at home?

These questions may seem trivial, but since there is so much about you I must keep secret, those details will make the difference between others believing you are

real and not just a figment of my imagination.
Please write.

Shalom,
Trudi

▼▼▼

When I heard nothing for another ten days, I convinced myself he was all right, just too busy to write, and tried to think of a way to push the envelope a bit further.

My own daughter-in-law, the daughter of a Holocaust survivor whom my son married after divorcing his first, non-Jewish wife, had brought a Jewish atmosphere into his home and taught us all about many Jewish traditions and observances. Since our family had become a melting pot of different religions, inviting both Jewish and non-Jewish guests to join us for family seders quickly became part of our tradition.

Thursday, March 25, 1999
Dear Simon,

I don't know if you have returned from your trip, but I trust your lectures went well.
   I am writing to invite you to my family's seder on April 1.
   Matthew seemed to enjoy coming to many such occasions at our home and always felt safe. So, since you seem to be able to travel quite easily, if you can get away, we would love to have you. . . .
Let me know.

Write when you can.
Trudi

▼▼▼

CHAPTER SEVEN

Thursday, March 25, 1999
Trudi,

I just arrived home thirty minutes ago. Everything went well, thank you.

I cannot free myself to attend any extra activities when I travel because there is usually someone traveling with me.

Also, I travel with exactly the money they give me for my expenses, and I have to account for everything I spend.

You have to understand that while I serve in the priesthood I depend economically on the Central Church. They pay my salary, my expenses, etc. The only money I have for myself is saved for a serious event: if I must disappear one of these days.

I felt sad reading your last letter. If they [the publishers] think I am a figment of your imagination, let them know this: you have a pretty good imagination!

We will meet one of these days. Just give it time. It has to be done carefully, for my protection. Anyway, thanks for the invitation, and one of these days, I will attend.

Please write.
Simon

▼▼▼

Simon's letter puzzled me. It did not fit the picture of his life as he had occasionally painted it for me. I had gotten the impression he was living a fairly independent life, free to travel quite often, and I felt uncomfortable with the gnawing suspicion he might have been lying to me.

Friday, March 26, 1999
Dear Simon,

I am sorry you cannot come to our seder. For some reason I assumed you were

Chapter Seven

*sometimes free to travel alone, for leisure, like to Canada to see the snow, to _____
, to smuggle out your friend, to _____, for the bullfights, and to Spain, to visit
your mother.*

*You once told me you were able to let go of your priestly persona, to be your real
Jewish self, and I was happy for you, relieved to know you have brief moments of
normalcy. Now you sound like you are a prisoner, saving money for your escape someday.*

*About the publishers turning down my manuscript, don't worry, I am working
on other sources. This book will be published someday, I promise. And when I get
money for it, I will share some of it with you, as I did with Matthew.*

Simon, do not despair. Someday things will be different.

*In the meantime, you can feel some comfort knowing you are doing something
important to help your people. Perhaps it will not be asked of you that you do it all
your life.*

Shalom,
Trudi

▼▼▼

Friday, March 26, 1999
Trudi,

I am glad to hear from you.

My biggest problem is that I have to account for every penny I spend.

*When I went to Canada, to see the snow, they paid my flight, my hotel,
and they always knew where I was.*

*When I went to the Vatican, there always were others traveling with me,
and they only left me alone to go to Spain because they knew I was visiting
my mother.*

*Yes, there are times when I can get away alone, BUT ONLY AFTER
TAKING A LOT OF PRECAUTIONS . . . then I can have the chance to
be normal. . . . BUT IT HAS TO BE DONE VERY CAREFULLY.*

CHAPTER SEVEN

After years of practice, I have learned to perfection how to disappear, how to be somewhere without being noticed, how to check my surroundings, etc. Of course, after so many years my superiors trust me, but inside the Church, you never can be sure.

Please don't give me any money. I can't accept it.

Let me know how I can help you. And please, send me questions.

Let's start again.
Simon

I wrote to wish him happy Passover, "a safe place to celebrate . . . at least a good meal."

It took three more letters to get a response.

Wednesday, March 31, 1999
Dear Simon,

You must be busy with Holy Week, a hard time for you, I bet.

Holy Week always brings back a lot of memories for me. I remember how I felt once I had finally decided to give up Catholicism, how part of me still believed I might end up damned for all eternity if I left!

Despite my fear, I was determined to make a break. So I made it official by committing the ultimate sin: going to Easter mass and taking communion without first going to confession. Then I dared G-d to strike me dead on the spot and send me straight to hell!

After fifteen minutes I walked out of church and haven't been back since.

Do you have a VCR? I just saw a remarkable film by a Brazilian director, Hector Babenco, about a group of missionaries who go to the Amazon to convert the native "savages" AT PLAY IN THE FIELDS OF THE LORD. It shows the failure of their efforts and the price paid by everyone . . . mostly the Indians. . . . If you have a chance to see it, let me know what you think.

Chapter Seven

I know this is a crazy, aimlessly rambling letter, but when there is a lot of time between your letters I always start to be concerned about your safety, and my connection with you becomes fragmented.

Take care, and write when you can,
Trudi

▼▼▼

Wednesday, March 31, 1999
Trudi,

You are right, this is a hard time for me. As a matter of fact, I have to travel to _____, to assist in the General Mass there. Damn that!
Speaking of VCRs, yes, I do have one. Every week I rent a movie. I am a fan of actors like Mastroianni, Alain Delon, J. P. Belmondo, Sofia Loren, Vittorio Gassman. I love European films. I find them more serious, more artistic, more profound. A simple movie that deals with real situations of human life is beautiful . . . but no movies for me this week!

Take care.
I will write when I get back next week.
Simon

▼▼▼

Monday, April 5, 1999
Dear Simon,

I hope you got through last week OK. I can only imagine what that must have been like for you.
Here is another thing we have in common: European films and bullfights! We'll talk about this another time.

Can you tell me what your duties are as a priest? Do you ever have to give sermons?

When you lecture at a university, what subject do you teach? Has anybody ever challenged your authority or expressed suspicion?

When you get back, please answer as much about this as you can. Every little bit of information helps.

Trudi

▼▼▼

Monday, April 5, 1999
Trudi,

I'm back. I will help you as much as I can.

Remember, despite the fact that I own a personal computer, I have to be careful every time I check this e-mail account. Time has taught me to avoid any situation that might create suspicion from people around me.

After I read your letter I erase it immediately. (What if someone steals my password, for example?) For every question, every detail you write, I have to rely on my mind to remember.

My life is the same as that of any person involved in the field of religion. I have to present myself as a person who believes 100 percent in Catholic dogma, who appreciates the life style, morals, and values held by the Catholic Church.

I am involved in the Eucharistic function, academic duties, and sociocommunal issues. All this is done to cover my real function: it is a necessary mask that protects the real ME.

He went on to reiterate again that the priesthood was only a cover, a way to fulfill his duties to his people.

Someday I want to be a rabbi for my people. I have to rest now.
I will chat with you more. . . .

Simon

Chapter Seven

Reading this letter, more than ever before, I could feel him squirm, his intense discomfort at having to spell out the full range of his priestly duties. It is as though the very thought of describing it all made him gag!

Instead of saying: "I have to say daily mass and give communion," he hid the meaning of that task behind the generic, and hopefully vague term: "Eucharistic function."

"Academic duties" probably meant teaching catechism, dogma, and confirmation classes to children and conversion classes for adults, theology at seminaries and universities.

"Sociocommunal issues" most likely involved pastoral counseling. What that must have cost him emotionally!

I understood the euphemisms behind which he tried to hide his daily regimen, having lived as a Catholic in a convent school for so many years, but I did not want to assume anything for my research and needed him to be more specific in his own words.

Friday, April 9, 1999
Dear Simon,

I can see that sharing details about certain parts of your life is very difficult for you. Are you afraid someone will catch you in the act of writing, or is it the subject itself you cannot bear to elaborate on?

You do not have to justify over and over again why you are wearing your priestly mask. Anyone reading your letters would have no doubt where your own spiritual commitment lies, and what you hope to give to your people.

But if I were to interview you in person, as I usually do when I do research, I would remind you that I, myself, can provide the generalities, while what I need from you are the personal details, the small specifics that help make the accounts believable, authentic.

I would ask you to elaborate, be less abstract, more concrete, to make the facts of your life come alive for the readers, who are most likely to be other Jews. They will not know what you are talking about when you use terms like "Eucharistic function."

I WANT THEM TO UNDERSTAND, FEEL, HEAR, SMELL, TASTE WHAT THE LIFE OF A CRYPTO-JEWISH PRIEST IS LIKE, AND WHY HE LIVES IT!

As long as you remain anonymous, couldn't you take them with you behind your mask, let them feel the fear, the conflict, the spiritual soul split you have to endure, the price you pay every day of your life? Could you not show them how you cope with it, how you keep your Jewish soul intact while you live this life?

I keep wondering, IS THERE ANYONE THERE FOR YOU while you wrestle with all this???

I am grateful you are willing to struggle with these painful issues.

Shalom,
Trudi

▼▼▼

In Simon's next letter (also dated Friday, April 9, 1999, which I inserted out of sequence earlier), he finally went into great detail about his life at the seminary, how his grandfather brought him to Spain at age twelve to attend Catholic boarding school for three years while teaching him to be a secret Jew on weekends.

He described how he felt reciting Catholic prayers and attending mass and how happy he was each Friday when he could welcome the Shabbat with his beloved grandfather.

The letter ended abruptly, explaining he could not bear to go on with the account because *"too many memories are coming alive."*

Later, when I asked for more details about some facts that seemed to conflict, he elaborated on his relationship with his grandfather.

Chapter Seven

Monday, April 12, 1999
Trudi,

Regarding your questions: I am sorry for not being more specific. I will explain everything according to my capabilities.

Please remember I have not spoken about these facts in many years. The people who live around me know another story, one I made up to cover myself.

Please remember that all the time I have to live keeping checking behind my back.

If it sometimes looks like I try to avoid specific dates, locations, events, it is because I was taught to do it.

I have trained myself to speak in a free way without revealing who I really am. It is hard to tell somebody my real story, not because I don't trust you, but because I do not speak so open with any other person, so please be patient with me. I will do my best.

We never attended a secret Jewish service during our time in Spain. My grandfather wanted to keep the image of good Catholics.

But in our small apartment there was a hidden mezuzah in the door, a menorah in the living room, candles for celebrating the Shabbat, and a round table where we sat to eat the special bread.

There was a lot of joy in my heart every Friday afternoon . . . and you see, Trudi, it is in this way that the words of the prophets came true: YOU WILL CELEBRATE THE SABBATH WITH JOY, YOU AND YOURS.

Since my grandfather and uncle are both dead now, there is no one left: no one else knows that I am a Jew.

Stay well,
Simon

▼▼▼

In one of my letters I related that my brother's grandson, who was having his bar mitzvah atop Masada in Israel (a fortress where one thousand Jewish men, women, and children rebelled against their Roman oppressors in 66 C.E. and chose suicide rather than risk being captured), was the very first child in my family to celebrate this important event.

When I did not get a speedy response and continued to prod him with more questions, Simon became annoyed with me:

> *Wednesday, April 21, 1999*
> *Trudi,*
>
> *I'm OK. It just happens I have a lot of work to do. The Church, the regional Church Council, the theology classes at the university, other seminars out of the country, and the normal duties every priest has.*
> *I will write as soon as I can!*
> *Remember, I also like to take appropriate time to answer all your questions, and when I have seven or eight things on my mind, I cannot think very well.*
> *Congratulations on the bar mitzvah. What a privilege!*
>
> *Anyway, take care,*
> *Simon*

▼▼▼

I realized I was pushing him too hard, so I wrote to apologize.

No reaction for two weeks.

> *Sunday, May 2, 1999*
> *Trudi!!*
>
> *Well, finally my schedule is more flexible. I have moved out of town to rest for a couple of days. I was so busy I did not even get to see any of the Sevilla bullfights!*

Chapter Seven

Please send me more questions and I will take time to deal with them.

Shalom,
Simon

▼▼▼

Wednesday, May 5, 1999
Dear Simon,

Sorry you missed the bullfights. Were you in Spain again, or do you watch the corridas on TV?

My last questions before you got so busy were:

When you go out of town to lecture, who is the audience? Seminarians? University students? What subjects do you teach?

I am trying to get some idea of the role you play with your own people.

What sorts of problems do they ask you to help with? Is it mostly security matters or personal issues, like spiritual, religious, marital concerns?

With whom do you socialize? Do you have friends with whom you are comfortable, with whom you can be your real self?

I am trying to show you are a real, breathing human being, not just some cold statistic defined only by facts and numbers. That is the reason for the more intimate, personal questions.

Don't worry, I will know how to disguise any identifying details. Remember, I have a Marrana soul, so I, too, know how to hide.

Enough for now, I am glad we are back on track.

Shalom,
Trudi

▼▼▼

What I really wanted to ask was: "Did you ever have a girlfriend? Have you ever had sex? Do you have to lead a celibate life?" But I did not feel the time was right for such intimate inquiries. . . .

Someday, maybe.

Despite his offer to get back to work with me, several subsequent letters from Simon failed to relate to most of my questions. He sounded distracted, preoccupied.

Then I received a letter that explained why.

Monday, May 17, 1999
Trudi,

My mother died yesterday. So I will have to travel to Spain.

My mother died alone because I decided to live this life. My goal is to bring peace and comfort to those who suffer, and I couldn't even be with my own mother!

The same happened with my grandfather and my uncle. I spend my life with those I don't really know, and those who know and love me cannot receive my love.

I am going away for a while. I am thinking of breaking my vows.

I hope this does not affect your project. Please, as a friend, keep my identity a secret. I don't need any more pain. If I survive, I will come back.

Your friend,
Simon

▼▼▼

The letter stunned me. Simon never expressed so much pain before.

I immediately wrote to offer my condolences. I sent another letter the next day, asking him to clarify what he meant by "breaking my vows." Did he mean he was thinking of giving up the priesthood?

Only then did it occur to me I might never hear from Simon again.

Chapter Seven

Tuesday, May 18, 1999
Dear Simon,

I wrote you yesterday, feeling your sadness, your despair, and all I wanted was to comfort you.

Now I feel my own sadness at the thought of losing touch with you.

You have become like family to me. I had hoped to meet you personally someday. You have inspired me with your courage, your devotion, and I hoped you would remain part of my life.

Now I am afraid it all might end this way, with you in so much pain, sounding so hopeless.

I hope you will write me once more before you leave or perhaps from Spain. Please let me know you are all right, safe.

Besides the personal loss, I am also sad because, of course, this is bound to affect my work, which I had hoped might help bring about some changes, would help your people.

There is so much more I wanted to ask, understand, explore with you.

Maybe, someday, somewhere, we can meet.

G-dspeed, Simon, and stay safe.

Shalom,
Trudi

P.S. By the way, The Mezuzah will finally be published in Spanish by Siglo XX, a good Madrid publisher!

The next weeks were again filled with anxiety, concern over Simon's safety.

I kept sending messages of encouragement and support almost daily, offered any help he might need, hoping he would somehow find a way to pick up his e-mail, from wherever he might be.

Finally, after three weeks of silence, a short letter.

CHAPTER SEVEN

Friday, June 4, 1999
Trudi,

I'm OK. Thanks a lot for your concerns. I am still in Spain since the death of my mother.

I have given up the priesthood. I am no longer a member of the Church. I am better now.

I will travel to New York in July and stay there a couple of weeks. If you want, we can meet there.

Simon

I reread his letter again and again: Simon was not only safe, but he was actually offering to meet with me!

Best of all, it seemed he would have a normal life after all, as normal as a Crypto-Jew's life could ever be! Or was he perhaps ready to come out openly as a Jew?

My head was buzzing with questions: What were his plans, where would he live, how would he support himself, how did the Church authorities react, did he tell them his plans or did he just walk away?

Did my constant prodding to justify his life as a secret priest have anything to do with his decision? All those questions would have to wait until we were face-to-face.

I wrote him that I would be in New York a day or so in August on my way to a wedding in Boston. Would he be able to make it around that later date?

Monday, June 7, 1999
Trudi,
If you want to talk with me in person, I am open. I will come later. Contact me during your stay in New York. It would be nice if you could stay an extra time during this trip so we can meet.

Chapter Seven

I am glad to hear about the Spanish version of your book. Finally!

Take care.
Simon

▼▼▼

In the next letter I tried to pin him down to give me some indication about where I could reach him in New York, but he wasn't ready for that.

Tuesday, June 8, 1999
Trudi,

When the time comes, send me an e-mail and tell me where you would like to meet and at what time. We could meet in the lobby of your hotel.

We can meet one day, have lunch, and talk. I will love to respond to all your questions in order to help you with your research.

However, I want you to know that, after this, I will disappear and make a new life for myself, far from my past.

Hope to see you.

Simon

▼▼▼

The fact that he was about to cut off should not have surprised me. After all, he had warned me about that before, but the reality of his intention nevertheless gave me a jolt.

I consoled myself with the hope that once we were face-to-face, I would be able to convince him to stay connected.

I wrote to give him details of where I was planning to stay in New York and when.

In my next letter I gave in to my growing anxiety.

CHAPTER SEVEN

Tuesday, June 8, 1999
Dear Simon,

I am sorry to hear you are planning to disappear after our meeting. I had hoped we might continue to work together while keeping your identity and whereabouts secret just as I did for Matthew . . . FOREVER.

I would be terribly disappointed if our work would end prematurely. You encouraged me to tell the world about Crypto-Jews, in order to convince mainstream Jews to accept you as Jews, to help bring about some understanding, some healing.

You have given me invaluable information to accomplish this, and I have always been committed to our task. But I can only complete this with YOUR help, with YOUR voice, with YOUR experience. The work is far from finished.

Although I know I have no right to ask you do anything you don't want to do, I sincerely hope you will stay in touch even after you "disappear."

In the meantime I look forward to meeting you face-to-face at last.

I can only imagine how scary this transition must be for you. I wish I could help. Let me know if there is there anything you need.

Shalom,
Trudi

▼▼▼

Next day I finally added what I should have expressed earlier:

Wednesday, June 9, 1999
Dear Simon,

With the surprise of hearing everything you told me, I forgot to tell you that although I know how hard this decision must have been for you, I am glad you are finally going to be able to live the normal life you left behind ten years ago.

You deserve to have an easier life!

See you soon.
Trudi

Chapter Seven

The next letter threw me off balance.

Thursday, June 10, 1999
Trudi,

Due to my health condition, all I can offer you is one day. However, I will do my best. For sure we will meet on August 16 in New York.

Hope to see you soon.
Simon

WHAT KIND OF HEALTH CONDITION?

Was he gay? Did he have AIDS? I had to quickly check my tendency to catastrophize and reminded myself that, although sometimes I tend to over-react emotionally, at heart I am an optimist.

I wrote to tell Simon I hoped he would soon feel better and asked again if he needed any help.

When I heard nothing for another three weeks, I grew increasingly concerned.

Monday, July 5, 1999
Trudi,

Thanks for all your concerns. My health is better. I was able to survive the crisis because of my good basic physical condition and I have just left the hospital. That is why I haven't written these last few days.

In second place, I am happy to announce that I will get married, to the same girl I had to leave when I entered the seminary! (I was very young at that time, but she was my girlfriend.)

And now, after all these years we will get married!

Simon

CHAPTER SEVEN

Before I could express my joy at Simon's news, there was another short note written the same day:

> *Monday, July 5, 1999*
> *Trudi!*
>
> *Can you believe I will marry the only girl I ever dated in my life! Amazing, isn't it?*
>> *Take care.*
>> *G-d bless you for all your support!*
>
> *Simon*

CHAPTER EIGHT

So Simon would get to live a normal life after all, with someone to be close to, someone to love him!

At first I had felt a little concerned about having pressured Simon to defend his life as a priest, secretly praying that someday he would quit, but now I felt G-d had not only heard my prayers, but probably had this in mind for Simon all along!

I kept waiting for him to confirm the arrangements for our meeting in New York. I was also excited at the thought of perhaps meeting his future wife.

Since in his delirium of contemplating his new life he did not take the time to elaborate on his future plans, I felt it safe to assume that coming to New York meant he must be planning to return to his secret Jewish community in Latin America.

After all, there no longer was anyone in Spain who knew about his real identity, no more Jewish relatives, and no Jewish community there for him to minister to.

When I heard nothing for two weeks, I convinced myself he and his bride had gotten married and were on their honeymoon, and rejoiced in that thought.

I bought a lovely silver filigree mezuzah made in Israel for the young couple as a wedding gift, one similar to the first one I ever owned.

Later I also found a small pictorial magnet to hold notes on their refrigerator door, created by a talented Crypto-Jewish artist, depicting a bride and groom under a khuppah (a canopy covering the bridal couple during Jewish wedding ceremonies) with a rabbi performing the secret ritual.

When I had still heard nothing from Simon ten days before our scheduled meeting, I wrote him again, to make sure our plans were still on track.

By now it was an effort to keep dark thoughts from invading my mind, but I kept counteracting them with a vision of Simon and his lovely bride happily together and too busy making love to be bothered with anything else.

I offered Simon all possible ways to reach me in Boston, where I would be attending a wedding with relatives. I was looking forward to our meeting on August 16.

From August 8 to 11, 1999, Los Angeles hosted the eighth annual conference of the Society of Crypto-Judaic Studies, at which I was scheduled to read a few of our letters for a presentation called "Correspondence with a Crypto-Jewish Priest," the first public exposure of my research.

After the lecture, which was received with great interest and emotional response by the assembled scholars and researchers, I ended my talk by excitedly announcing I would be meeting Simon in New York exactly one week later.

I returned home and checked my e-mail. A letter from Simon appeared in my mailbox, dated August 4.

This was August 9! His letter was written and dated five days earlier! Such a delay had never occurred before. Why now? How did it happen?

Wednesday, August 4, 1999
Trudi,

I am sorry for not writing before, I couldn't.

I have not been married. My fiancée was in an automobile accident on the road to _____. A drunk driver hit her and her car was destroyed.

The damage to her brain has been terrible and the doctors said there was nothing they could do.

What can I say? Is this the life I deserve? Is this my punishment for leaving my "call"? What is it? Why has this happened just when I was close to finding a new life?

If I can, I will travel to New York, but right now I am destroyed.

Sorry
Simon

Chapter Eight

What kind of cruel joke was this?

And for what mysterious reason did Simon's letter show up in my mailbox five days after he sent it, although I had been checking my e-mail several times a day?

I reread the letter again and again, wondering why such a tragedy should have happened just when Simon was so full of joy and anticipation.

I was also afraid he would assume I did not care about his tragedy when he did not hear from me for days after he told me what happened. How would I explain why I had not immediately written to comfort him?

Monday, August 9, 1999
Dear Simon,

I don't know why, but I only just NOW received your terrible letter!

My G-d, I am so very sorry, and only wish there were something I could do.

Please do not think this happened because you left the Church. You did the right thing . . . you were meant to be a Jew, and G-d meant for you to be a Jew.

I have no answers, only that G-d sometimes allows things to happen for reasons that we don't understand. . . . May he give you the strength to survive this and may he send you healing for your heart.

Simon, you are a very special person. Do not give up hope, please.

And please, let me try to help even if now it looks that nothing can help.

I send you my prayers.
Trudi

He wrote the same day. Our letters must have crossed.

CHAPTER EIGHT

Monday, August 9, 1999

The person I loved is gone . . . dead. As simple as that . . .

There is nothing you can do, Trudi. Don't worry about me. I have a place to stay and I have money. But my heart is broken.

Again.

Simon

▼▼▼

Tuesday, August 10, 1999
Dear Simon,

I am so sorry, so sad for you.

Please do not think this is punishment from G-d. IT IS NOT! This is a time to grieve, and I grieve for you, with you . . . and I feel helpless.

A short while ago a gunman broke into a school at a Jewish community center near where I live. Did G-d want to punish the six small children who were shot? Or their families? NO, NO!

Fate is a random thing . . . unconnected to G-d's will or judgment. What happened to you and your love is a tragedy, a horribly unfair accident affecting everyone connected to you and to her, but there is no one to blame except the drunk driver!

Do not torment yourself with thoughts that only fill you with despair.

I hope you are with people who can comfort you, give you warmth and care, so you can express your grief openly and safely.

Please stay in touch.
Trudi

▼▼▼

I kept hoping against hope that Simon would keep our date, but he did not meet me in New York.

I thought I might find a letter from him when I returned from the wedding, but there was nothing.

Adding to my concern and sadness in the weeks that followed was the fact that some of my colleagues, who had heard me talk at the Crypto-Jewish conference and later called full of anticipation to get an update on my meeting with Simon, expressed their suspicions that the accident probably never happened and that Simon made up that terrible story in order to avoid meeting me face-to-face.

"Don't we all know that Crypto-Jews always lie?" they said.

I remembered how Matthew had made it clear that the way secret Jews have survived years of scrutiny and persecution was by subterfuge.

Had the prospect of being with me in person become too close for Simon's comfort?

I had to admit that this was possible.

Aware of my bias, I carefully considered but soon dismissed this skepticism as unwarranted.

I examined the essence of our connection and reminded myself that those who voiced their suspicions and doubts had heard only a small sampling of our letters and could not possibly have had a sufficiently broad overview of our relationship on which to base a valid judgment about Simon.

Looking back on our fourteen-month-long dialogue, I asked myself, What might be his reason for lying to me, for ensnaring me in a fantasy? How would he have benefited?

After all, he insisted on remaining anonymous. He refused my offer to share any money I would earn if my book about him were ever published. He was determined to avoid personal publicity, was not looking for fame . . . so what would have been in it for him?

Despite his fear, Simon had been so eager to cooperate, so willing to be open with information about his people no still-hidden Jew had ever risked revealing. Did it make sense he would be so devious now?

What's more, when Simon sought me out initially, he had expressed surprise that I had bothered to respond to his letter. Clearly he never expected, any more than I did, what would result from that initial exchange.

Then, not long after we began writing, Simon expressed regret at having missed a chance to arrange a meeting with me when both of us happened to be in Spain at the same time.

Now it was Simon himself who proposed that we meet in New York. Yes, he might have gotten cold feet at the last minute, but it is unlikely he would have tempted fate to get out of meeting with me by fabricating such a terrible story.

After several weeks of silence, I began to fear that I would never hear from Simon again. I had invested over a year in my work with him, and now it looked as though he had decided to disappear before we could finish our task.

After a while my sensitivity to the turmoil Simon was going through became blunted.

I lost sight of the monumental spiritual and physical changes he had to be dealing with, now that he had burned all his bridges behind him by cutting himself off from the Church as well as his community after losing his mother, followed so soon by the sudden death of his first and only love.

Focusing on my own needs, I wrote a letter I wish I had never sent.

Tuesday, August 24, 1999
Dear Simon,

I hope these past weeks have brought you some measure of peace and healing.

This is a very hard letter for me to write. If my friendship means anything to you, you will respond.

Matthew, the priest in my book whose story prompted you to write to me, was someone I met in person.

He trusted me with very personal information, and I never betrayed him. I never revealed any of the sensitive details to my publisher, but I was able to tell my agent I had proof, and that was enough: they trusted me because they knew I had a reputation as a researcher to protect.

I have loved working with you these many months. I have never doubted any-

thing you have told me.

BUT THAT IS NOT ENOUGH.

I must have something from you to substantiate what you have told me. Meeting you in New York, seeing you in person would have accomplished that to a great degree: you would have become a real person, not just an Internet ghost. As it is, what proof can I offer?

Please write.

Trudi

▼▼▼

The minute I sent off the letter, I regretted it.

I wrote again, to apologize for pressuring and trying to manipulate him, but he did not respond.

By the time I had spent the next two months writing him every few days, sending him words of encouragement, offering help, support, sharing news, I reluctantly accepted the fact that I had caused Simon to cut off, that I would never hear from him again. I decided to give it one last try.

Monday, October 25, 1999

Dear Simon,

Just returned from New Mexico, where I gave four talks. Beautiful country, lots of Crypto-Jewish history. I was interviewed by a formerly hidden Jew, Lorenzo Dominguez, who has a radio program in Santa Fe devoted to secret Jewish issues, called "Mi Seferino."

Today is my birthday, and I hoped I would find news from you that you are well and safe. . . .

I think of you often and send you my prayers and wishes for blessings.

Shalom,

Trudi

CHAPTER EIGHT

Half an hour later Simon replied!

Monday, October 25, 1999
Happy birthday, my dear Trudi!

As for me, I am OK. I have learned to suffer my pain in solitude. I am trying to rebuild my life and forget the past.

Shalom.
Simon

Tuesday, October 26, 1999
Dear Simon,

Thank you for the nicest birthday present!
  I am so glad you are alive and getting on with your life.
  I will continue to pray for your wounds to heal and for your life to become fulfilling and safe. . . . I know you will not always be alone. . . .
  Be well, my dear friend, and please stay in touch.

Shalom,
Trudi

I did not dare hope his one letter meant our correspondence would resume. Simon was clearly still in deep mourning, and I certainly understood his need to put the past behind him. I had learned my lesson and was relieved to have gotten another chance. . . .

Chapter Eight

Then came another short note, with a surprise attachment.

Tuesday, November 2, 1999
Trudi,

This is a picture I took with my fiancée a couple of days before she died.
    I wanted you to see who I am and what I had: the chance for a normal life.

Your friend,
Simon

▼▼▼

There, looking out at me from the monitor, was a color photo of Simon and his lovely girl: he, a chubby-faced young man with curly black hair, a sensuous mouth, intense dark eyes with a brooding expression, dressed in a suit and tie.

She was the typical Spanish beauty, with long dark hair, perfect skin and teeth, wearing a pearl necklace and matching earrings, her face wreathed in a bright smile.

I looked at the photo for a long time: here was Simon at last . . . not in the flesh, but no longer a ghost.

Although he missed meeting me in person, he wanted to show me who he was, that he was real.

Tuesday, November 2, 1999
Dear Simon,

Thank you for your short note, but especially the photo of you and your lovely girl . . . she was really beautiful, and I feel so sad seeing you together. But it is nice to see what you look like . . . you are very handsome.

    It is far too soon for you to talk about a normal life. You are still in too much pain . . . you need time to heal. But you will not stay alone forever, trust me on that.

I don't have a clue where you are. Still in Spain? If so I will be there next spring, to speak to my Spanish publishers and convince them to bring me there for a book tour to promote their new edition when it comes out, so I need to brush up on my español!

Please stay in touch, and thanks again for sending the photo.

Shalom,
Trudi

▼▼▼

Simon answered right away.

Tuesday, November 2, 1999
Trudi,

Well, you can practice your Spanish with me if you want.

Thank you for your comments on my physical appearance . . . my mirror thanks you.

I am in Europe, but not in Spain. I have started a new life. I have a job teaching at the university, I have an apartment, and everything is going OK . . . but the pain is there.

I am not attending temple or mass. . . . I can't.

Simon

▼▼▼

Wednesday, November 3, 1999
Dear Simon,

When you say you are not able to attend any religious services, I can really connect to what you are feeling. . . .

Chapter Eight

It is hard to forgive a G-d who has allowed so much tragedy to happen. I too have often felt that way. But as a Jew, I can at least scream my anguish and rage at G-d.

Do you still feel you are in danger and need to be afraid? With the kind of life you have lived, fear must have become so much a part of your reality, you probably cannot imagine living without it.

I hope someday you will feel safe enough to let go of it. Please write whenever you feel like talking.

Shalom,
Trudi

▼▼▼

No news for the next three weeks. So I wrote again.

Thursday, November 25, 1999
Dear Simon,

Today is Thanksgiving. Last year you wrote that you were spending that day with American friends. I hope that this year you are not alone, also with friends.

Among the many things I am thankful for this year is your generosity in sharing so much of your life with me. . . . I know how hard this has been for you, but I hope that you too have derived some benefit from our serious explorations, despite the pain and fear.

I hope that wherever you are, your heart is beginning to heal a little. I hope you have friends or family nearby with whom you can be yourself, free from danger, starting to rebuild your life from the ashes of the past.

I send you good thoughts, and prayers for blessings and healing.

Shalom,
Trudi

▼▼▼

Minutes later Simon responded.

Trudi,

Yes, today is Thanksgiving . . . a time to give thanks for the good things we have . . . and once had. . . .

Be well.
Simon

▼▼▼

Now I was beginning to relax a bit, feeling that perhaps things between Simon and me were going back to some semblance of normalcy: no questions and answers yet, but at least a resumption of a slow rhythm in our communications.

Friday, December 3, 1999
Dear Simon,

Tonight is Hanukkah. I send you wishes for fulfillment of all your new dreams. . . .
I hope you have made new friends and that you find your work meaningful.
Please let me know how you are.

Shalom,
Trudi

▼▼▼

Sunday, December 5, 1999
Trudi,

My only hope is that the lights of the miracle may bring happiness and new light into my life.

Chapter Eight

For now, I have no place to celebrate Hanukkah since the local synagogue is close to the university where I teach . . . that, by the way, is a Catholic university.

But I'm OK. Thanks a lot for your concern.

Your friend,
Simon

▼▼▼

I stared at the letter, unable to believe what I read.

Like a newly released convict who quickly commits a crime because he does not know how to cope with life outside of jail, Simon seemed incapable of letting go of his self-imposed spiritual prison, unable to live a free, Jewish life!

I waited nearly a week before responding, afraid to let my feelings show. But time did not diminish the intensity of my dismay.

Saturday, December 11, 1999
Dear Simon,

Your last letter left me feeling sad.

I had hoped that, now that you are no longer a member of the clergy, you could finally live a normal life, free from fear or the need to hide, openly Jewish, balancing your inner and outer lives. But that clearly is not yet possible.

I can only assume that the reason you took a position teaching at a Catholic university is because that is where your past experience lies. Perhaps they know you and offered you a job.

But I wonder if the Crypto-Jewish lifestyle is so much a part of you that despite the fact that you have said it is hard and sad, you cannot let go of it.

Is this so? Or is the fact that you still have Catholic family in Spain the reason you cannot come out into the light? Are you close to any of them?

I know that someday you will have what your innermost soul longs for, as impossible as this may still seem to you. You are still too close to your tragedies to believe in miracles as I do.

Do you have anyone nearby in whom you can confide, someone you can trust? I miss our discussions.

Remember, you once wrote you got as much out of our dialogue as I, that it was a "two-way street"? I hope that someday soon you will be ready to resume our exploration. . . .

Is there anything I can do for you? Let me know. Stay well, and please, stay in touch.

Shalom,
Trudi

I should have known the effect my letter would have on Simon. I should have recognized my implied judgment and contained my anxiety, but as before, my impatient self took over and obscured Simon's need to adjust to his new life slowly.

I was in a hurry for him . . . but he wasn't ready to be free . . . or happy.

I realized all that as soon as I sent off the letter . . . but by then it was too late.

I wrote again and again, pleading for him to not just disappear.

During the next six months I received just one short note from Simon, in response to my question in a letter dated June 13, 2000:

Are we no longer friends?

His answer came the next day, June 14, 2000:

Chapter Eight

Dear Trudi,

Of course we are still friends! Never doubt that. I just want to forget my past and what I am. I want to start over and move on.

Simon

▼▼▼

I still hear from Simon every now and then. In one letter, dated January 2, 2001, he sounded lost, depressed, rootless and admitted he was *"tired of living. . . ."*

I worry about him but feel that eventually he will find his way. And, perhaps, someday we will reestablish our relationship.

But even if Simon decides to put all elements of his past life behind him and never gets in touch again, what he has given me is invaluable. For now, I am grateful for everything he has been willing to share, grateful he revealed so many secrets of his soul.

Now what he needs is time to heal.

I can wait.

And hope.

Postscript

January 2002

Until recently, the little notes I occasionally got from Simon, just to let me know he is alive, contained nothing of substance.

The fact that I was unable to reveal Simon's true identity caused my manuscript to be rejected by several publishers. When my book was finally seriously considered for publication by a university press, I had not heard from Simon in five months. This caused an expert on the history of Crypto-Jews, who was selected to evaluate my book for the faculty review board before they would accept it, to express concern over Simon's apparent disappearance. How could I get him to reconfirm his earlier permission to have his letters published if he was gone?

The expert also voiced serious skepticism about the very existence of Crypto-Jewish priests, since in all his own research he had seen *"NO examples of this from the fifteenth through seventeenth centuries. It seems to me to be a myth and of fairly recent origin."*

Reading this expert's comments and doubts, the university faculty review board now began to reconsider the risk of publishing my work.

Then, as has happened so many times before after a lengthy silence, Simon reestablished contact with me and sent four letters spaced over a two-week period, precisely during the time these critical deliberations were going on. He had been away, he explained, lecturing at various universities in Latin America, away from his computer, and had just gotten back. When I told him my book was finally being considered for publication, he wrote, in part:

Postscript

Tuesday, November 6, 2001
Dear Trudi,

About the book, well, you have been fighting for that and I am happy to hear your effort is "creating fruits" [sic]! Good, at last. I trust again your work will help people understand my story, and the story of many others.

This seemed to alleviate the publisher's concerns about obtaining Simon's release. Any remaining doubts about the authenticity of Crypto-Jewish priests also appeared to have been relieved by a passage relating to that subject that Dr. Stanley Hordes had come across in his own research and that he was kind enough to pass on to me.

In *Los Judios en el Reino de Galicia* (Madrid Editora Nacional, 1981, pp. 465–67) Dr. Hordes found a section titled "Multitud de Converses en la Iglesia," where the large presence of conversos in the priesthood is discussed. It cites such authorities as Antonio Dominguez Ortiz and Julio Caro Baroja and offers examples found in various religious orders.

Translated by me from the original Spanish, Dr. Hordes quoted: "It was not rare to find that many were judaizing (practiced Judaism in secret). A well-known case was that of Franciscan friar Antonio Mendez, a judaizer and protector of other judaizers, who perished in an auto-da-fé in Santiago de Compostela on October 18, 1631. He was not the only judaizer. Others were accused of heresy, being conjurers and practitioners of witchcraft. There were many more such cases."

Since you, my dear reader, hold in your hands proof that my manuscript was eventually accepted for publication, despite many still unanswered questions, it is now up to you to decide whether you believe what Simon and I wrote is true or not.

Postscript

So, what lessons can be drawn from an exploration into this Crypto-Jewish priest's soul?

Anyone concerned with the corrosive effect of prejudice, of racial, ethnic, and religious discrimination and the misuse of power by one group over another, whom it has judged to be "less than" its own, should wonder how many others, not just hidden Jews, are secretly, silently suffering a similar fate . . . and worry about who could be next.

What stands out for me is the increased awareness of the terrible price paid by all who have been forced to hide their true identity. Whether it is to escape life-threatening persecution or to better their position in a world that arbitrarily excludes some of us from a fair participation in society, denial of an essential part of self almost always results in a crippling of the soul. At its worst, it eventually becomes something akin to spiritual suicide.

I have always believed that any people as persecuted by so many others throughout the ages as the Jews must have learned something from history and, remembering our own pain, would never knowingly allow the same agony to be inflicted on others. This, I felt, would make us no better than those who have deprived and tormented us.

While recent circumstances have seriously challenged those beliefs, I still fundamentally hold on to their essential truth.

Of course, all of us have the right to defend ourselves if we are attacked. But when, in order to achieve security, we allow others to be oppressed, without remembering the pain of our own oppression, when we misinterpret "chosenness" to justify depriving others of their basic rights as human beings, we only perpetuate their hatred and obsession with revenge, with both sides propelled into an ever-escalating competition.

If we do not break this deadly cycle with renewed determination to find creative nonviolent solutions, how can we hope to bring about healing not only to our own people, but to our whole wounded, war-torn planet?

If we give up trying, the persecuted, displaced, and disowned among us will continue to feel that hiding their true self and assuming false identities offer them the only hope for survival.

I take comfort from catching occasional glimpses of brave forays into peaceful coexistence in some of the most unlikely places, where tolerance of our diversity and acceptance of our differences are respected and honored and healing follows.

1. The Abraham Fund supports Israeli kindergartens attended by both Arab and Jewish children. This experiment, ongoing for many years, has confirmed that when barriers are removed early enough, before hatred has hardened, friendships can flourish and emotional and political enmities are less likely to take root. Promoting peaceful coexistence is the primary purpose of these kindergartens.

2. In Neve Shalom's Peace Village in Israel, young Arab and Jewish children have lived and studied together in harmony for years. Recent news revealed that the village's financial support, especially from America, has been greatly reduced because of the growing violence in the area.

3. Here in the United States, a summer camp called Seeds of Peace was founded by John Wallach in 1993. Although he first focused on the Middle East, bringing Israeli and Palestinian teenagers to spend a few weeks together in Maine, Wallach recently expanded his efforts to include a small number of American campers with youngsters from other conflict-ridden regions: the Balkans, Afghanistan, Pakistan, India, Egypt, and Cyprus.

In a recent article in the *Los Angeles Times* called "My Friend, the Enemy," Ruth Ellenson quotes Wallach: "When a foreign government chooses the kids who attend 'Seeds of Peace,' they usually reflect that government's point of view, and are not the ones who want to make peace.

"At the beginning, each side sees themselves as victim and the other as aggressor.

"The first week they are either completely idealistic or convinced that their point of view is the only right one.

"The second week they begin to see that the version of history they have been taught may not be the only reality there is, but also come to realize there are very real reasons for the hate that exists between the two sides.

"By the third week they know they have to deal with the hatred and still need to accept each other anyway."

Mistrustful and hostile when they first meet, filled with old memories and preconceived notions inherited from their families, they often return home transformed, even as friends.

Sadly, some of the participants recently admitted that back home, with hostilities escalating daily, they have to hide their newfound friendships, pretend they were not affected by everything they experienced and learned here, or risk being considered traitors by their own people.

In "My Friend, the Enemy," Ellenson quotes Susan Crais Hovanec, a member of the South Asian Bureau of the U.S. State Department:

> "No one suggests that youth exchange is going to end a war or conflict. Children born of despair, violence, and intolerance are nurtured to hate and mistrust. They are highly susceptible to terrorist propaganda. But children who experience cross-cultural encounters for themselves form their own opinions and become 'seeds of peace.' The hope is they will be less vulnerable to being recruited into terrorist organizations."

4. Even at the height of the Intifada, Hadassah Hospital in Jerusalem uses its fully integrated staff of Arabs and Jews to treat all patients with equal care, including offering transplants to anyone in need, without regard to the donors' or recipients' racial or religious identities.

5. Harold Schulweis, the senior rabbi at Valley Beth Shalom in Encino, California, where I occasionally attend services, has long been one of the most active religious leaders committed to introducing creative ecumenical measures.

Because he is a prolific author, brilliant scholar, and lecturer, his actions and innovative proposals have significantly influenced not only the conservative Jewish community he serves, but leaders of other faiths.

Despite initial opposition from his congregation, he was the first to successfully challenge his fellow Jews to acknowledge our debt to Christian rescuers who had risked their lives to shelter thousands of Jews threatened with arrest and deportation during the Holocaust. Years ago, long before others recognized their responsibility to help sustain those heroic non-Jews, who were often shunned by their own people and lived in dire circumstances, Rabbi Schulweis established The Jewish Foundation for the Righteous, which provides ongoing financial assistance to more than sixteen hundred aged and needy rescuers in twenty-seven countries. Its educational programs include seminars and curricula for junior and senior high school students that teach the values of moral courage based on the witnessed events of altruistic behavior.

In addition to establishing a yearly ceremony to honor such Holocaust Rescuer Nations as Spain, Denmark, and Bulgaria, Rabbi Schulweis also organized a series of dialogues between Conservative, Reform, Reconstructionist, and Orthodox Jewish rabbis and arranged lectures by spiritual leaders representing Moslem, Protestant, Buddhist, and Catholic points of view. The attendance at these events exceeded everyone's most optimistic expectations as hundreds overflowed the sanctuary.

To the consternation of some members of his congregation, Rabbi Schulweis visited a local mosque and invited its Moslem clergyman to attend services at his synagogue shortly after the September 11, 2001 attack on New York City's World Trade Center, in an effort to counteract a growing groundswell of anti–Arab/Moslem fervor.

Like Rabbi Schulweis, Rabbi Allen Freehling of University Synagogue in Westwood, California, has for some time been sponsoring highly controversial and often contentious Jewish-Moslem dialogues. Such acts of moral courage are examples of the kind of activism that have inspired others to join these religious leaders in their quest for harmony and peace.

7. Whenever I think of rotund Señor Doroteo, whom I interviewed in Spain in 1991, I smile. We met at a Torah class taught by a Catholic nun at a Madrid convent.

The three nuns who lived at the convent were Sisters of Zion, an order founded by a priest who was a Jewish convert who nevertheless felt an obligation to counteract the anti-Semitism of the Church perpetuated in its traditional Catholic catechisms.

Among the courses offered at the convent by the nuns as well as Catholic and Jewish visiting scholars was the study of the Hebrew language, the history of the Jews in Spain, and an exploration of the effect of Jewish culture on their own, stressing the enormous contributions by Jewish writers, philosophers, and scholars. The people of Madrid responded with ever-growing interest, and the classes were always packed.

The nuns were active members of Amistad Judio-Cristiana, an organization whose Jewish and Christian members began fifty years ago, even while Fascist dictator Franco was in power, to devote themselves to teaching Spaniards about their country's Jewish heritage. Today, nearly thirty years since Franco's death, such courses are routinely offered in Spain's public schools and universities.

Señor Doroteo, a sixty-five-year-old deeply devout Catholic layman who discovered as a boy that he had Jewish ancestors, found a very personal way to accomplish the Amistad's goal: after traveling to Palestine in 1939 to see for himself if all the terrible things he was taught about Jews were true, he fell in love with the country and its people.

Since then, for years, he has been spending his meager savings to take groups of Spanish children to Israel to "show them what real Jews are like," adding: "I love Jews because Our Lord was a Jew."

6. For two years I participated in a dialogue between Second Generation, a group of adult children of Jewish Holocaust survivors, and adult children of German and Austrian World War II survivors, some of whom had been Nazis. It was sponsored by the University of Southern California and cofounded by a German-born professor who became an anti-Hitler activist when he discovered his father was a Nazi.

The well-trained group leader encouraged us to express our feelings freely, short of physical violence. As expected, sparks often flew as memories awoke and loyalties clashed.

After spending years in therapy dealing with my survivor guilt and my rage at the Nazis, I thought I had come to terms with those feelings to the point of relative inner calm. Participating in the German-Jewish Dialogue showed me that buried attitudes can spring to life with unexpected passion.

During one session the participants were asked to talk about what our parents told us about their own war experiences. It was not surprising that most of the Jews admitted that our parents had volunteered little about their past, reluctant to dredge up memories of their time spent in camps or in hiding, claiming it was all still too painful to talk about.

The German participants spoke mostly about their families' accounts of suffering through bombings, displacement, hunger, cold, and other dangers and deprivations.

I listened calmly, until one young woman described her parents' reactions upon returning to their ancestral home in East Germany after the country's unification, only to find another family had appropriated it in their absence.

"Can you imagine how it feels to find strangers living in your own family home?" she asked.

Something inside me snapped.

"How would you like to return to find your home burned to the ground by your neighbors who betrayed you to the enemy, with nothing left but your family's bones in the ashes?" I screamed.

Shocked at my outburst, I covered my face with my hands, waiting for the group's reaction: I was expecting the Germans' self-righteous, accusatory defenses: "You Jews are not the only ones who suffered! We, too, lost loved ones. We, too, were bombed, hungry, hounded, afraid. . . ."

I was prepared to shout back: "But you started it all!"

But that is not what happened. All that followed my outburst was silence.

Then I felt the touch of a hand on mine. I looked down to find a blond, blue-eyed young German woman kneeling at my feet, tears in her eyes. She put her arms around me and whispered: "You have a right to your anger. If I were a Jew, I would feel the same way. . . ."

I felt heard. My anger melted. Our group ended that session sobered and more deeply connected than when we began. There was hope for healing.

7. But my most personally affecting and meaningful experience happened when I was sent by the United Jewish Communities Speakers Bureau to address 150 members of an international baccalaureate class at a Wichita, Kansas, public high school.

"There are just five Jews in that whole school," I was told. "They should hear your story."

I found it refreshing to meet with and respond to these bright, curious, intellectually and emotionally open young people who posed questions Jewish audiences seldom ask.

Although I could have spent another hour discussing the ethical and spiritual issues involved and exploring the emotional consequences of hiding one's true identity, I finally had to cut off the dialogue to catch my plane home.

As I packed up to leave, a young girl came up to the podium.

"Can I tell you a secret?" she asked in an almost inaudible voice.

When I nodded, she came up close and whispered in my ear: "I am a Jew. I've never told anyone. Now I will."

Back to Simon.

How have I been affected by this extraordinary epistolary relationship with him? What has been the impact on my soul, on my own Jewishness, as I witnessed his spiritual struggle to hold on to his Crypto-Jewish identity and traditions as the only surviving Jew in a family of Catholics, working in a Catholic world while pretending to be one of them?

The most powerful consequence of this experience has been the renewed and intensified focus on a conflict I thought I had put to rest: long ago, as a child, I did not know I was born a Jew. After I found out, I lived as a Catholic for years. Eventually I searched for and reconnected to my lost roots. Now I live as a Jew. Period.

End of story?

Not yet.

My correspondence with Simon revealed that the spiritual and psychological issues with which both of us were dealing are deeper and far more complex than I realized or wanted to admit, and my inner conflict is far from resolved.

There are many things about being Jewish I love. I am full of admiration at our people's traditional dedication to action, our emphasis on learning, on living virtuous, ethical, and charitable lives.

I am proud of the enormous contributions, far greater, proportionally, than our numbers would lead anyone to expect, that Jews have made to society, in science, philosophy, and literature, among other cultural areas.

I love that the Talmud is so respectful. It offers us Jews choices. Each page has wide margins. The center portion tells about Jewish laws and commandments, and the margins quote commentaries of renowned Jewish scholars to show the many ways those precepts might be interpreted.

As a Jew I am allowed to argue with G-d. We are not only permitted to challenge, to question controversial religious or philosophical issues, but are actually encouraged to engage in critical dialogues with each other and our rabbis!

As a people, there is so much diversity in our tribe that none of us should ever need to fear having our identities as Jews questioned by other Jews. We should feel safe in the belief that there will always be a place somewhere among our own where we can feel at home. But Matthew, Simon, and I found out that this is not always so.

Although I know I am a Jew, my dialogue with Simon has made me aware that I have not yet fully integrated a secure feeling of "belonging." Surrounded now by Jews who have always known who they are, I keenly feel the absence of Jewish traditions passed down from generation to generation, of familiarity with Jewish ritual, of growing up Jewish.

My mother was ninety-two years old when she was invited to her first ·seder. With wonder in her voice she later called to tell me how even toddlers participated in the traditional holiday festivities:

"Imagine, such small children . . . and they read Hebrew, they knew all about the history . . . they knew what to do. . . ."

Then she grew quiet for a moment before going on.

Postscript

"I guess you can't pass on something if you've never had it. . . ."

Without an anchor to a Jewish past, I still feel emotionally adrift, not quite certain I have a solid spiritual ground beneath my feet.

So much of my non-Jewish past still lingers nostalgically in my memory. I miss the personal, more tangible relationship to G-d that Catholicism seemed to offer during my formative and most impressionable years, especially at times when Jewish teachings feel cold, intellectual, and abstract by comparison, with so much emphasis on THE LAW.

Torah classes have often left me troubled over the frequent instances of violence, the emphasis on G-d's wrathful justice, instead of love, compassion, forgiveness as stressed in the Beatitudes and the Sermon on the Mount.

Although I am a committed Jew and would never go back, could never again accept Catholic dogma, I do remember how I felt as a child attending mass, being inspired by Jesus' words, stories of his miracles and the selfless deeds of some of the saints.

I remember how I felt receiving the communion wafer during mass when I actually believed a tangible, living G-d was inside me. And I recall the serenity and peacefulness of singing Gregorian chants and sharing silence with fellow students and nuns during school retreats when I felt transported to another reality where I felt deeply connected in spirit not only to G-d, but to the whole universe.

All that feels lost now. And I miss it.

Yes, of course I am only too aware of how the Church twisted and misinterpreted Jesus' words and intentions into rigid decrees and used them to justify terrible persecutions against Jews and anyone else considered to be an infidel: the Crusades, the Inquisition, the pogroms, the clergy's silence during the Holocaust and, most recently, during ethnic-cleansing massacres in the former Yugoslavia and Rwanda, among others.

I know, too, that many saints were canonized precisely because they sought martyrdom defending their faith by murdering Jews. The fact that there is talk of canonizing Queen Isabella and Pope Pius XII is evidence that the Church still believes that those proving their devotion to their faith by ridding the world of "heretics" by force or by inciting and condoning their persecution deserve a halo.

I recognize all this intellectually, but what I am responding to here is a spiritually starved child's memory of a time when the world had exploded in unprecedented violence, when a Catholic country provided a safe haven to my family and a convent offered me time for peaceful contemplation and refuge from the turmoil around me.

I realize upon reflection with benefit of hindsight, now that some time has passed with only an occasional word from Simon, that what I hoped to get from my connection with him was to feel about my own Jewishness the way he feels about his.

I wish I could have had a relationship with a grandparent like the one who so lovingly taught him how to be a Jew. I long to experience the joy he felt, the beauty, mysticism, and meaning with which his Jewish practices and traditions enriched his life. I thought I could get all that by absorbing his psyche, by somehow integrating his soul through his letters, allowing myself to be filled and nourished by them.

What I should have known, and what I have had to learn over and over again from my sometimes obsessive dialogue with Simon, is that I cannot expect to get to that secure inner place through someone else's experience, that I must find a way to tap into a connection with my Jewish self some-where deep inside my own Marrana soul.

I recognize now how much I projected on Simon, how deeply I identi-fied with him. Wanting him to give up his Catholic cover became impor-tant to me because I unconsciously believed I needed him to be uncontami-nated by Catholicism in order to be rid of that contamination in myself, so I could be wholly, unconflictedly Jewish.

What I failed to see was that he was able to maintain his inner Jewish integrity and that, even as a Catholic priest, he was less affected and infected by Catholicism than I still am.

Among the many things I learned from Simon was that conflict is an essential part of an examined life. It can kill us if we ignore or fail to grapple

Postscript

with it. But if we face the conflict, it will test us, hone us, and force us to make conscious choices. What Simon showed me was that conflict does not preclude a deep commitment to our chosen spiritual path. It defines us.

In order to live that commitment as deeply and radiantly as Simon, until tragedy plunged him into despair, I will have to continue to search, to question, to struggle, to fight my inner demons until I find my own relationship to my Jewish G-d, to my Jewish identity.

I deeply believe that with G-d's help, Simon will find his way to wherever he feels his heart and spirit lead him, and perhaps someday choose to live an openly Jewish life.

Meantime, the memory of his shining, searching soul will serve as a bright beacon to light my own path.

Addendum

March 2002

After a four-month-long silence, Simon once more reestablished contact.

The first letter was a short note letting me know that he had recently accepted a full-time teaching position at a university in Latin America. He added that he had just returned from a trip to Israel.

I was happy to hear from him and glad I had not known he was going to be in Israel at the height of Palestinian terrorism. I would have worried until I knew he was back safely. I congratulated him on his new job and asked how it felt to be in Israel.

He answered quickly.

As always, his words seemed mysteriously connected to my own inner process. But this time there was a profound difference. They almost sounded like an epitaph.

Monday, March 25, 2002
Trudi,

My experience in Israel was great. Nothing more beautiful than to see the lights of Tel Aviv at night, the cafés, the people outside, the music, the culture . . . a piece of Europe in the Middle East.

My experience was also ecumenical. I had the chance to attend different religious services and it was interesting to see that every religious expression holds a part of the truth: proof of man's need for a deeper answer.

Many things have changed for me the last year. I have come to understand that it would be impossible to obtain recognition as a Jew unless I agree to conversion. However, I also understand that my identity means more and is more powerful than a bunch of regulations created by man. My sense now is to promote an ecumenical spirit, tolerance between different religions, and warn of the danger of imposing anyone's will on others. It feels beautiful to be capable of attending any religious service, and experience the beauty of rituals and the mystical sense of religion without placing an emphasis on who are the chosen ones and who are not chosen. . . .

I am OK. My life has a purpose again, as a man, as a member of the human race, as the descendent of converted Jews with a tradition and a lesson from history.

Stay well.
Simon

▼▼▼

Although Simon sounded more serene, less stressed than he had for a long time, his letter left me strangely sad. In my mind's eye I saw him drifting from one spiritual discipline to another, drawing some sustenance from each but committed to none. Would Simon never feel he really belonged anywhere? Had he given up hope? Had I been too optimistic, too naive in my belief that he would ever try to live an openly Jewish life, maintain his commitment to his Jewish self?

Nevertheless, I felt glad he appeared to have emerged from his depression at last, relieved that he was safe, finally settled into his new life, ready to embark on a potentially fulfilling new spiritual mission.

On March 26, the day before Passover, I wrote to wish him happy holidays, told him about the finalization of my book contract, reassured him that I had kept his identity hidden, and asked him if he would like to share whatever royalties might accrue from the book sales. I also mentioned I hoped he would tell me more about his visit to Israel.

As he had done the last time, he answered almost immediately.
Wednesday, March 27, 2002
Trudi,

Addendum

Try to picture a person like myself, with all my historical background, approaching the Western Wall.

Nobody asks me if I am converted or if I am "a son of the covenant." I am wearing my yarmulke, my tallith is under my arm, and as I approach the Wall, I put it on myself and out loud I start to pray . . . but when I get there my mouth can hardly repeat "Shema Israel."

My dream as a secret Jew, as a Marrano, has been accomplished: for a couple of minutes I was just one more Jew back home, no questions asked.

I went to Tel Aviv, stayed there five days, then traveled to Eilat, stayed five more days, then finally I came to Jerusalem. There, I attended different services: a Catholic mass, a Protestant service at the garden tomb, and finally services at a Sephardic synagogue in the Old City.

I don't want any money related with book sales. It is enough for me to know that you would keep my identity secret, because there are many things about my past, my secret life, my heritage that would hurt me if they came to be known. Your friendship is more than enough. You have helped me more than you can ever imagine by telling the story, and that is the best payment.

You see, the seder does not end with remembering the Jews coming out of Egypt. It would be fulfilled if all Jews, spiritually or physically, might come back to Eretz Israel and be restored. The biggest question to be answered during the four years of our communication remains: Who is a Jew? And this is up to G-d . . . not to man.

Shalom,
Simon